Our Egalitarian Universe

Our Egalitarian Universe

Arpit Chaturvedi

KALPAZ

ISBN: 978-93-5128-160-3

Price : ₹ 250

First Published, 2016

Published by

Kalpaz Publications
C-30, Satyawati Nagar,
Delhi – 110052
E-mail: kalpaz@hotmail.com
Ph.: 9212142040

Printed at: G. Print Process, Delhi

Cataloging in Publication Data—DK
Courtesy: D.K. Agencies (P) Ltd. <docinfo@dkagencies.com>

Chaturvedi, Arpit, author.
Our egalitarian universe? / Arpit Chaturvedi.
pages cm
Includes bibliographical references.
ISBN 9789351281603

1. Equality—India. 2. Equality. I. Title.

HM821.C43 2015 DDC 305.0954 23

Dedicated to all Indians (of the past, present and future)...

Contents

Foreword

After going through the manuscript of the instant magnum opus of braintickling dissertation brilliantly produced by a spring chicken Mr Arpit Chaturvedi, devoted to the FOUR VEDAS, as his name suggests, evokes rather compels the mind to focus rapt attention to vistas of virgin, hut trenchant thinking, reasoning and approach leading to loadstar directing to the societal weal, the resultant end produce of which may be egalitarianism ordained by the Grand Architect, Geometrician and hitherto unchallenged Craftsman Almighty,

Tautly scripted, Mr Chaturvedi's book, "Our Egalitarian Universe", is divided into Four Chapters of which Chapter One and Chapter Two deal with casteism and communalism, the twin evils of the society. He concludes that these are culture-based problems in the society.

Absolute classlessness in the society, neutrality is myth. He has very rightly pointed out so while tracing the evolution of class or classes, Various factors emerging from time to time alongwith the development have always obliged the formation of classes imperative in Chapter Three. Even the sages, scholars, thinkers and observers of theology classified - SPIRIT, SOUL SUPERSOUL and BODY. All living beings have founded groups for their protection. The call for protection is innate. Right to five is not the grant by any power body or law document. Such bodies or documents only recognised and protected.

In concluding Chapter Mr Chaturvedi recognises aeons old accepted conclusion "that change is the only constant in this universe" and it dovetails in the theme of the book.

In summation, "Our Egalitarian Universe" oozes vivacity and energy, acuity, profound scholarship encompassing an infinite spectrum of mesmerizing and fathomless ocean of craving for knowledge.

I sanguinely believe that the level of the research work of the author, effort and the quality of critical evaluation of the subject has earned a glittering welcome and magnificent reception in the world of dedicated inquisitive researchers in the field.

In the end I wish and yearn very best for the book as well as the author and his future ventures.

(D. S. SINHA)
Former Chief Justice
Dr Justice Gujarat &
Former Chairperson
The Gujarat State Human Rights Commission

Preface

Our Egalitarian Universe (OEU) is a series of reflections on the questions that have haunted the mind of every Indian and perhaps of every person in the world. The possibility of equality or egalitarianism is the underlying theme in all the essays in this book. As we grow up, equality is something that one yearns for and an egalitarian society is something that we all hold as the 'right' kind of society to live in. However, soon enough, as a person gains more consciousness of the world an ever broadening crevice creeps up in what we consider as the 'right' type of society and what it actually is. The realisation of the fundamental inequity comes by looking around and through experience. The fact that equality is not a reality around us while inequality is comes as a disorienting experience, which either leaves people coping up in a number of ways that range from becoming quixotic to becoming overtly non-egalitarian in their world view – keeping a balance amidst overwhelming circumstances, naturally becomes difficult. OEU is an attempt to ask and at times answer questions such as:

"Do we live in an equal society?"

"Is an egalitarian society possible?"

"If yes, then how?" or "to what extent?"

"What is the role of an individual in creating such a society? What is my role? What can we do?"

The first two chapters deal with the caste and communal disturbances in the Indian society and answers the question "Do we live in an equal society?" in non-affirmative.

The third chapter discussed the problems of casteism and communalism further and submits that all casteism, communalism, racialism etc. are essentially different forms of separatism in the form of inter-group conflicts. The third chapter then moves on to discuss conditions through which such inter-group conflicts can be resolved and proactively avoided. The third chapter already answers or rather assumes the answer to the question of "Is an egalitarian society possible?" to be in affirmative.

The fourth chapter puts forward a postulate that "we are living in times where the degree of equality is increasing". At the same time, this chapter acknowledges the role of superordinate historical forces that impact the degree of inequality prevalent in the society, which also means that the current trend of growing equality may be reversed before we know it! This chapter visits the question about the possibility of an egalitarian society again and evaluates the conditions under which such a society may be possible answering the question of "to what extent can egalitarianism prevail?" It concludes that an absolutely egalitarian society can only be possible in conditions which are extremely difficult to achieve and a society can merely strive towards equality without however arriving an absolute state. Just like a market can strive towards becoming a perfect competition market. Nevertheless, such a conclusion is not seen in a pessimistic light as the possibility of 'almost' being in an absolutely equal state does exist.

The fifth chapter then moves on to discuss the nature of power, firstly by stripping the concept of power of any moral connotations and taking it as any other natural force or rather social force. It also tracks a cyclical course in which power changes its form. Secondly, this chapter argues that the presence of power does not essentially mean the absence of equality, on the other hand, power is the determining factor that decides whether the society will have equality or not, depending upon the number and disposition of the people who hold power. This chapter also corroborates with the idea of the coming of a new era but rejects the idea that it will come through the utter destruction of the old era, rather it holds the view that it would emanate from the old era. Certain elements of the past will indeed be done away with, but many, such as the presence of a competitive and progressive commercial sphere, will be retained.

The sixth chapter answers the questions: "What is the role of an individual in creating such a society?" "What is my role?" "What can we do?" It begins with establishing that notwithstanding or rather in proper consideration of the course of history, human beings have been able to steer the society towards more egalitarian shores. It takes the example of Mahatma Gandhi who was able to do so and was also able to diminish the presence and the impact of fault lines in the society that manifested itself in forms of caste, communal, regional and linguistic conflicts. Finally, it is submitted in this chapter that a dynamic leadership style that takes into consideration the historical forces and environmental realities is most effective in doing away with socio-economic discord. In this chapter, it is also argued that Mahatma Gandhi was indeed a person who had power, but his power was a moral and a dynamic one that was directed for the strengthening rather than the dissolution of the social fabric. Hence, the essential quest for power has been viewed between two groups – group +ve (people who strive towards unification or people who consider power as a means to an end) and group –ve (people who strive towards politics or people who take power to be the end in itself). Who decides if a certain group is group +ve or a group –veis based on the perspective of the people. At best, what can be submitted is that if there are two groups, both of which are striving to give privileges to a certain section of the society and deny the same to others, then both the groups are group '–ve's. On the other hand, if there is a group that strives to give equal opportunity to all, is essentially one that could be categorised as 'group +ve'.

Finally, the last chapter which comprises of the appendix was found to be important to convey a key message that concerns the purpose of this book; the message being that a consciousness, exposure and understanding of the 'other' is a prime determinant in creating a society which is egalitarian in its mindset. This essay was written with the combined efforts of a friend – Upasana Singh (her effort in the same being greater than mine) to drive home the point that in the global community that we live in, there is a greater need for laws and lawmakers to be exposed and become more accepting of different cultures, different mindsets, as well as different needs of different peoples.

A note on style

It is a book of essays, a writing style that is meant to promote independent thought and hence I have been careful enough in making sure that as much as possible, I depend upon the works of others in forming arguments. Aldous Huxley has rightly commented that "the essay is a literary device for saying almost everything about almost anything" and his advice has been 'almost' followed in writing these essays. Finally, as the word 'essay' connotes, this work is an effort, a coming together of fluid ideas that change in interaction with the outer world. In fact, considering this a humble attempt at common-placing ideas admixed with the audacity to publish them, would not be an exaggeration.

As far as possible, quoting the exact sources of ideas has been diligently attempted. However, at times the same may not have been possible and an admission of tacit, but by no means inconsiderable, influences is only appropriate here.

Acknowledgements

A great many people have contributed in making this book possible.To begin with, I would like to thank my teachers who have taken the effort to give shape to my ideas -this book is nothing but reflections on the knowledge handed down by some of the distinguished minds in the Indian academia and their influence on the thought of a student. These teachers include Mr Pramod Sharma, Mr Akash Pradhan, Mr Mayank Bhatnagar, Dr Firdos Anwar, Mr Sanjay Varma, Mr Saroj Jha, Dr K.S. Subramanian, Ms. Vidya Moorthy, and Late Dr Bipan Chandra – who over the course of telephonic conversations left an indelible impact on my mind and mentors (Dr P.L. Punia, Dr Smita Chaudhri, Mr. Yashwant Mahadik, Ms Chaitali Mukherjee, Dr Rekha Dwivedi Mr Premraj Pillai, Dr Rajsekhar Krishnan). who helped me see the practical side of things and allowed me opportunities to work for worthy causes that lent insight as well as experience in putting thoughts to practice Also, I would like to thank my family members (Late Sh. Sushil Chandra Chaturvedi, Sh. Ashoke Chaturvedi, Smt. Rajani Chaturvedi, Dr Apurv Chaturvedi, Smt. Archana Chaturvedi, Sh. Atul Chaturvedi, Smt. Rachna Chaturvedi, Sh. Abhinav Chaturvedi, Smt. Neeta Chaturvedi, Mr Eeshan Chaturvedi, Ms. Eesha Chaturvedi, Ms. Aishwarya Chaturvedi and Mr Abhishtha Chaturvedi) who always extended support and encouragement to my endeavours even if they did not seem rational every time. Further, I would like to thank my friends and colleagues (Mr Ankur Arora, Mr Abishek Sharma, Mr Amit Sharma, Mr Rudhreesh Kapur, Ms. Upasana Singh, Mr Vishwaraj Singh, Mr Anubhav Agarwal, Mr Indra Shekhar Singh,

Mr Aditya Sharma, Mr Faraz Khan, Mr Anshul Kapur, Mr Ayush Jain, Mr Archit Sardiwal, Mr Syed Mafiz Kamal Onik, Mr Kshitij Jalori, Mr Vivasvat Pal, Mr Smarth Gupta, Mr Kartik Aggarwal, Mr Mohit Agarwal, Ms Megha Bhatia, Mr Tarun Kumar, Ms Sweena Sethi, Mr Idris Parekh, Mr Tejas Shinde, Mr Anirudh Sardiwal, Mr Parikshit Sridhar, Mr Rishab Maniklala and many others) who helped in various ways ranging from discussing ideas over long walks, challenging my viewpoints, and going through my work innumerable times to suggest improvements. Finally, a credit to libraries is due (Kirori Mal College Library, Faculty of Arts University of Delhi Library, Indian Law Institute Library, Symbiosis Centre for Management and Human Resource Development Library, National Commission for Scheduled Castes Library) for their invaluable inputs.

CHAPTER 1

Casteism: A Problem Bygone? Or a Way of Life?

In an article, K.B. Kenneth compares the social system with the biological mutation selection model implying the social system to be very similar to the biological organism. Such a comparison is also used by functionalist thinkers to describe the structure of the society– which is likened to a living person. If such a comparison is to be made, then the Indian society would seem like a human being that has caught multiple infections in its body, each infection corresponding to a crevice in the society that impedes its functioning. These crevices are – casteism, communalism, regionalism, linguistic conflicts and economic conflicts.

Casteism is one of the first infections that as a society India received - much before the advent of new religious conflicts, perhaps even before economic ones. The nation has learnt to live with these infections with the help of pain-killing drugs and sedatives which make one believe that the virus has left the system, while the reality is, that the virus is ever growing, feeding on the body. The pain does, however, re-emerge from time to time, but is ignored and controlled thanks to drug induced perceptual wellness.

The Government of India's Anthropological Survey of India, under the leadership of K.S. Singh, brought out a series of publications titled 'The People of India'. This project identified 2800 castes including 450 SC, 461 ST and 766 OBC. It concludes that, **"Caste continues to be the basic building brick of Indian society"**. Dr Ingole, a scholar of social sciences in Mumbai said: "This historic verdict of the Anthropological Survey of India project did not get any publicity in India's press because our ruling class is shy of admitting this fact which has made them the rulers" (Ingole). To put things in perspective the Joint Stakeholder's Report on "Caste Based Discrimination in India" (2012) submits basis its analysis of the National Crime Records Bureau data that "every 18 minutes a crime is committed against SCs; every day 27 atrocities against them, (3 rapes, 11 assaults and 13 murders); every week 5 of their homes or possessions burnt and 6 persons kidnapped or abducted" (p. 5).

In the face of other conflicts or infections, such as the religious and communal separatism, which have lately caught the centre-stage of the public attention, since they are fresh viruses injected into the system and due to the multitudes of riots and politicking that make up novel stories attracting media coverage, the conflict of caste has been downplayed by the media. Not to say that there has not been any caste based riots and violence (See **Attachment: A brief survey of Caste based violence over the decades).**

'Since our system has new viruses now, the old ones consequently do not bother as much' – is the kind of thinking which seems to have developed over the years. The bad news is that the virus of casteism, though old, is not dormant and our body has not been able to develop its immunity so as to fight this virus. At the same time, the virus has kept on feeding over the body for centuries now and has weakened its immune system in such a manner that as soon as the body attempts to take a leap of progress, the system breaks down and only marginal and lopsided progress is made.

Recently a show appeared on the Indian television–Satyamev Jayate–that caught the attention of the Indian audience by discussing a plethora of social issues. The show though having gained overall breakthrough success, failed to gain much audience attention on the issue of casteism and untouchability as the episode featuring this issue ranked second last in terms of TRP[1] ratings amongst its first ten episodes. Even the star studded movie–'Aarakshan' did not do well on the Bollywood box office. That the caste problem does not bother the Indian audience anymore is not tantamount to saying that the caste problem has relegated into oblivion and does not pester the Indian society any longer. In fact, it has become a sort of a hidden monster that perpetratesits chicanery in stealth and shows up at the surface only in form of scattered and seemingly disconnected instances.

To fight this evil, this disease of casteism, it is necessary to understand its nature and origins. There are a variety of arguments that are offered by social scientists, politicians and journalists in this regard. However, many a times the diagnosis of the disease has not been completely right and in order to understand the correct medication for the disease, its correct diagnosis, the real nature of the virus, has to be understood.

A Problem of Religion?

The first argument put forward by some social thinkers to explain the cause of casteism is the religious argument–that points all its guns towards the Hindu religion and claims that there is something in the religion that extolls division of the society on caste lines. Such an argument does not seem correct when evidence suggests that at the time of the early Vedic period, the concept of being 'born in a caste' had still not taken place and there was much occupational as well as social mobility. Consider, for example, the below lines taken from the Rig Veda that shows how in a family, there could be people practicing different occupations:

> "I am a poet, my father is a physician, and my mother is a grinder. Earning a livelihood through different means we live together..."
>
> —Rig Veda, 9.112.3

The lines mentioned in the Rigveda are a testimony to the fact that religious scriptures *per se,* were not designed in a manner so as to perpetuate a rigid caste system. In fact, untouchability in the essence of the Hindu religion does not exist. The term 'Shudra' "is mentioned for the first time in the Rig Veda in its tenth book, which is the latest addition" (Sharma R. S., 2005). The fact that the Rig Vedas were written over a long period of time (1500 BC to 1000 BC) and that the term Shudra did not appear in the same till its last book proves that there was nothing in the religious philosophy at its inception, that laid a foundation for caste based divide as it stands today.

In fact, if the problem of caste were essentially a religious factor, it should have vanished in the sections of societies which later on converted from Hinduism.

Professor M. Lal Goel has explained that in India:

> "Religious conversion leads to new castes. When a caste of weavers converts to Islam, a new caste group is born...Christians and Muslims in India do not escape caste divisions. Caste division is supposed to be an aspect only of Hinduism. But Christian and Muslim communities are divided into a number of sub-groups which function like sub-castes. Christians include Syrian Christians, Catholics, Protestants, Goan Christians, Adivasi Christians and are also divided by state and region. A Tamil Christian may have little in common with his compatriot in neighboring Kannada, much less in Delhi or Calcutta. Muslims are even more divided: Sunnis, Shias, Bohras, Khojas, Ismailies, Ahmediyas,Wahabis and so on. Christian and Muslim caste groups practice endogamy—Bohras would marry among Bohras and Catholics among Catholics" (Goel, 2014).

A similar explanation is furnished by Imtiaz Ahmed in his book 'Caste and Social Stratification among Muslims in India'. The following is an excerpt from Ahmed's book (1978):

> While there can be little doubt that the Koran recommends the egalitarian principle, actual practice among Muslim communities in different parts of the world falls short of the Koranic ideal. Particularly in India and Pakistan the Muslim society is clearly stratified. First, there is a line which divides the Ashraf from the Ajlaf: the former are high and the latter low. The Ashraf are further divided into four ranked sub-groups: Sayyad, Sheikh, Mughal and Pathan. Some would regard Muslim Rajputs as a fifth

sub-group of the Ashraf. The Ajlafare similarly sub-divided into a much larger number of groups. All these groups, the Ashraf and the Ajlaf are endogamous. Furthermore, they are hierarchically arranged in relation to one another, the Sayyads occupying the highest and the Sweepers the lowest position.

A recent event of caste based violence among the Muslim population of Bihar wherein two men named Akbar Ali and Mustafa Ansari were beaten by the upper caste Muslims bolster the argument of the pan religious casteist mind-set prevalent in India. "There have been continual tensions between the upper caste Muslims, comprising the Pathans and Sayyeds, and the Pasmanda Muslims, comprising various sub-castes" (Gaikwad R., 2012).

In fact, there has been a long running movement in India to include 'Dalit Christians' and 'Dalit Muslims' in the list of Scheduled Castes of the Constitution of India. A report to the National Commission for Minorities by scholars at the Department of Sociology University of Delhi has furnished data on the appalling conditions and discrimination against Dalit Muslims and Christians in India (Deshpande & Bapna, 2008). The report has compiled approximately 144 research studies by various researchers ranging from the 1970s to the early 2000s to form a list of the various: 'Forms of Caste Based Social Discrimination among Muslims and Christians in India' including 'untouchability'.

All this essentially reveals that even by converting from the religion *per se*, the caste issue does not dissipate, which means that there is something other than religion in this whole issue and to diagnose the caste issue as a religious problem would be erroneous because if one does so, the solution then would sound like this– remove Hinduism, castes will vanish. However, the research mentioned above shows that even for people who converted from Hinduism, the caste system still prevailed.

Just Politics

Many thinkers hold the view that the caste problem in India would have been a problem bygone had there not been such marked political interests competing with each other in the society. A special event that uncovers the fact that the society in India is still seen in caste terms is the event of the elections. During the elections, most parties primarily conduct their vote-bank segmentation in terms of caste segments. Even renowned magazines and newspapers do not hesitate to publish forecasts and opinion polls in caste terms, using caste segments as they are well aware of the Indian reality. During elections, both caste based appeasement and threatening increases as the contesting parties line up to draw the larger chunk of vote bank to their side. The eventual losers in the game are the depressed castes in the society. As rightly pointed out by Dr Giuseppe Scùto "Before, while and after elections are held, dalits are regularly intimidated, beaten up, murdered..." (Scuto, 2007-08). Since the depressed castes are already weak, and form a major proportion of the voting population, they are most susceptible to political manoeuvring and manipulation.

The "first past the post system" of elections has also been blamed for perpetuating caste based manoeuvring. According to this system, in a particular constituency, a candidate who gets more votes than other contestants wins the elections. What happens as a result is that at times the first-past-the-post system encourages tactical voting? Voters have an incentive to vote for one of the two candidates they predict are most likely to win, even if they would prefer another – a third - candidate to win, because a vote for any other candidate will likely be "wasted" and have no impact on the final result. This system also leads the contestants of the elections to play on 'caste-combinations'.

Let us understand this by way of an example. Let us assume a society with 5 castes namely: Caste A, Caste B, Caste C, Caste D and Caste E. Caste A is weary of Caste B and all the other castes are, let's say neutral to all the other castes.

Now elections are being held for a position in this society which are being contested by three candidates namely: C1 (the ugly), C2 (the bad), and C3 (the good). Let us suppose C2 is from Caste B of which Caste A is weary. Now if a candidate is able to show that he has one or two castes backing him up and he is 'in the fight', for example if C1 succeeds in showing that Caste C and Caste D are on his side, and these castes form a large chunk of the population (statistics are also manipulated by many such candidates), then members of Caste A will tend to align with C1, members of Caste B will get polarised towards C2 and a candidate, C3 even if he has the cleanest of image and track record, and even if he shows most capability, will be ignored and will be unable to 'enter the fight' and is bound to lose the election unless he plays the caste card. Hence, not the criteria of development but fear, many a times drives the voting pattern.

However, such caste based politicking is done by the politicians only because of the fact that caste is a sensitive crevice in the society, an old wound that is yet unhealed and can be played with for political benefit. Hence, caste based politicking is not the disease, but a symptom of the disease of the caste virus.

A Rural Problem?

Another argument that comes about – is that casteism is more of a rural than an urban phenomenon. If that is so then why are the literacy gaps among the scheduled caste population and the

	Overall Male Literacy (2001) per cent	*SC Male Literacy (2001) per cent*	*Literacy Gap Between overall Male and SC Male (2001) per cent points*
Rural	70.7	63.7	*7*
Urban	86.3	77.9	*8.4*
	Overall Male Literacy (2011) per cent	*SC Male Literacy (2011) per cent*	*Literacy Gap Between overall Male Literacy and SC Male Literacy (2011) per cent points*
Rural	77.2	72.6	*4.6*
Urban	88.8	83.3	*5.5*

(*Source:* Primary Census Abstract for Total population, Scheduled Castes and Scheduled Tribes, 2001 & 2011, Office of the Registrar General & Census Commissioner, India).

non-scheduled caste population higher in the urban areas, both for males and females than the rural areas as the below tables from the 2001 and 2011 census data suggest:

The above table clearly shows that as far as the male population is concerned, in 2001 the literacy gap between scheduled caste population and the total population in the rural areas was 7 per cent and the same in urban areas was 8.4 per cent. Similarly, the gap in 2011 was 4.6 per cent in rural areas and 5.5 per cent in urban areas. Similar trends emerge for the female population as well, as shown in the below table:

	Overall Female Literacy (2001) per cent	*SC Female Literacy (2001) per cent*	*Literacy Gap Between overall Female and SC Female (2001) per cent*
Rural	46.1	37.8	8.3
Urban	72.9	57.5	15.4
	Overall Female Literacy (2011) per cent	*SC Female Literacy (2011) per cent*	*Literacy Gap Between overall Female and SC Female (2001) per cent*
Rural	57.9	52.6	5.3
Urban	79.1	68.6	10.5

(Primary Census Abstract for Total population, Scheduled Castes and Scheduled Tribes, 2001 & 2011, Office of the Registrar General & Census Commissioner, India).

As far as the female population is concerned, in 2001 the literacy gap between scheduled caste population and the total population in the rural areas was 8.3 per cent and the same in urban areas was a phenomenal 15.4 per cent. Similarly, the gap in 2011 was 5.3 per cent in rural areas and 10.5 per cent in urban areas.

By looking at the above data, casteism seems to be more of an urban phenomenon than a rural one. Yet, such a contention also cannot be conclusively held when crime data is observed. If we rank the top 14 most populous states in terms of scheduled caste population in terms of 'rate' of crime committed against scheduled castes for each state on the y axis and the 'incidence' of crimes against the scheduled castes for the same states on the x axis, the graph would look like this[2]:

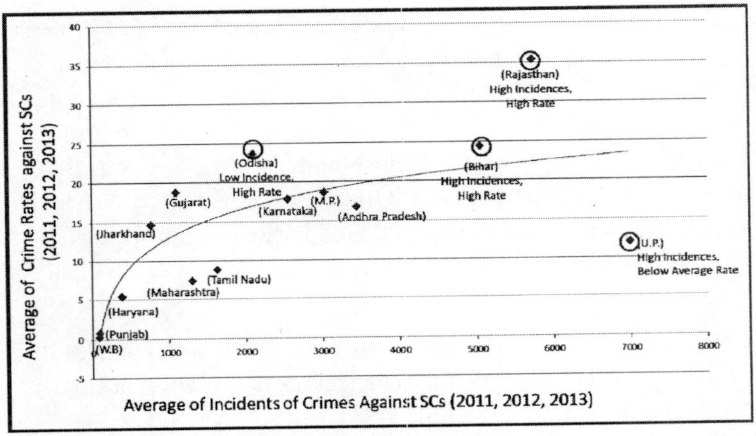

The above graph suggests that the more ruralised states such as Rajasthan and Bihar are more prone to caste-based crimes than the comparatively urban states like Punjab and Gujarat. Thus, basis the abovementioned graphs on literacy and atrocities committed against scheduled cates, no conclusive answer can be sought to resolve the issue of caste being either an urban or a rural phenomenon,Thus, perhaps it can be concluded that casteism is neither wholly a rural phenomenon, nor an urban one; in fact, it is widespread in the country in both urban as well as rural India.

Economics or Culture?

Another argument explaining the causation of the Casteist problem is the classic economic argument–that the caste problem grew as a result of inequitable division of surplus in the society[3]. The solution to the caste problem as per the supporters of this argument is naturally an economic one – give more money to the deprived castes and there shall be equality. While this may be a good formula to empower the depressed classes, this does not seem to be the final solution from the perspective of removing the caste based divide and rivalries from the society.

Smriti Sharma an economist at the Delhi School of Economics conducted a research on the hate crimes against members of the scheduled castes and scheduled tribes population in 415 districts spread over 18 states. Sharma related these hate crimes to the consumption patterns of the Scheduled Castes and Scheduled Tribes population vis-a-vis the non-SC/ST population. Sharma's research concludes that: "a widening of the gap in expenditures between the lower and upper castes is associated with a decrease in crimes committed by the upper castes against the SCs/STs". She adds that: "Moreover, this effect is driven by changes in the upper castes' economic well-being rather than changes in the economic position of the lower castes and tribes" (Sharma S. , 2013). The research finally submits the following:

> "We interpret this as the upper castes responding to changes in ***threat perception*** created by changes in the relative positions between the two groups" (2013).

With more money coming to one section of the society, the other section sees itself as relatively poorer and when the upper sections of the society lose their economic status they scapegoat the lower sections. Either way, an internecine warfare ensues. Hence, even with economic betterment of a section of the oppressed, the caste discrimination does not end.

The argument that the economic advancements for the Scheduled Caste can help change the situation of a socio-cultural bias against them does not arrive at the complete truth since it ignores the change required on the cultural level along with economic development. At times economic development, when not mediated by cultural acceptance (tolerance from other castes) can lead to a widening of the crevice of caste rivalries and can lead to violence. The following case is a testimony to the two converging trends– the occurrence of incidences of atrocities against the scheduled castes gaining economic power and their repression by the police (Subbiah M, B Malathi, 1971):

> Since 1980 the Dalits of Kodiyankulum village, in Tuticorin district, have benefited from the flow of funds from family members employed in Dubai, Kuwait, and the United States. On August 31, 1995, a 600-member police force attacked the all-Dalit village in the presence of the superintendent of police and the district collector and destroyed property worth hundreds of

thousands of rupees. In what appeared to be a premeditated attack, police destroyed consumer durables such as televisions, fans, tape-recorders, sewing machines, bicycles, agricultural implements, tractors and lorries, and also demolished food grain storages. They made a bonfire of clothes and burned the passports and testimonials of educated Dalit youth. The village post office was targeted, and police allegedly poisoned the only village well. A village elder claimed 'all through the operation, the policemen were showering abuse on us and made derogatory references to our caste, which only showed their deep-rooted prejudice.' District collector Paneerselvam, accused of leading the raid, was subsequently transferred to Madras. The stated purpose of the raid was to capture Dalits allegedly involved in the murder of three Thevars in a nearby village two days earlier. Many suspect that it was the relative affluence of the Dalits that attracted the attention of the uniformed men. The idea, it appears, was to destroy their economic base, because the police felt the Kodiyankulum Dalits provide moral and material support to the miscreants in surrounding areas. Similar raids have taken place during the southern district clashes.

Hence, empowerment which takes place in the background of mistrust and a threat perception creates further repression. Hence, it may be prudent to create a strong culture of tolerance while the empowerment for the depressed classes takes place. In essence, it is necessary to work on both the sides – the depressed and the others – in order to have a truly progressive social change.

Also, what happens at times when empowerment is not accompanied by a culture of tolerance is that when the sections of erstwhile oppressed get empowered, they begin oppressing those who are still in the shackles of backwardness. This has been pointed out by Ramachandra Guha while discussing atrocities that took place in the 1970s in Bihar in which the 'backward castes' inflicted suppression on the scheduled castes– both of these once on the receiving end of the social suppression, now were in a new position wherein the backward castes had asserted more economic power. It was now mostly the backward castes in Bihar that owned the land, and the scheduled castes who mostly laboured on it..."The backwards slipped easily into the shoes of the forwards whose lands they had gained. Like them, they treated the Harijans with disdain and often violated their women", noted Guha. One of the major example of such a social dynamics that led to suppression and violence was in Belchi, a village in Bihar where 'Backward Kurmis'...burnt 11 landless 'Dalits', the spark being a dispute over land. (Singh, 2009).

The examples discussed so far highlight two trends:

1. The trend of a cultural bias translating into an economic one
2. The trend of economic growth of dalits leading to an accentuation and/or re-activation of the cultural bias against them

The combination of the above two trends creates a vicious cycle and puts the Scheduled Castes in a "damned if you do and damned if you don't" kind of a situation. Here there seem to be two levers to deal with the situation– cultural and economic.

A final evidence for the argument that if, however, casteism were merely an economic issue specific to the Indian Sub-continent, the cases of caste discriminations should have ideally vanished among the Indian Sub-continent natives when taken out of their socio-economic setting. However, the case is not so. In the United Kingdom, a new debate emerged about whether to include caste based legislative protections in the Equality Act, 2010, which resulted in the an amendment to the Equality Bill, inserting a new provision (Waughray, 2009):

> Section 9 of the Act provides that a Minister may by order amend that section to provide for caste to be an aspect of race (and to provide for exceptions in the Act to apply, or not to apply, to caste).

At the same time, the U.K. Government decided that further research was needed in order to decide whether to exercise the power. In consequence, the U.K. Government Equalities Office commissioned the National Institute of Economic and Social Research (NIESR) to assess the nature, extent and severity of caste prejudice, discrimination and harassment in Britain and the implications for Government policy.

The National Institute of Economic and Social Research thereby conducted the research (2010) and has cited the following case among many others in its report[4]:

> The first time X knew anything about caste was at secondary school. Her friends had assumed she was of a higher caste and found out she was not.
>
> This led to bullying and rumour spreading: 'I lost so many friends and confidence, I couldn't focus on my work and it was just really bad for me'... She believes that the bullying was driven to some extent by the parents of pupils who said not to invite X to their home. There were others of the same caste in her school but they generally kept quiet about it. Some had a practice of 'hiding' their caste by not using their own surname but registering at the school as Singh or Kaur. In contrast, pupils of higher caste liked to 'brag about it'. It was considered 'cool' to be of higher caste and these pupils were more popular than others.
>
> ... X felt embarrassed and ashamed at having to state her caste in front of the class, and pupils were giggling at her response. X believes that the teacher did not realise that she had hurt her feelings....
>
> ... When she attends social events she is asked her caste by older women, which she believes is from interest in her as a potential marriage prospect...
>
> Comments by National Institute of Economic and Social Research (NIESR), United Kingdom:
>
> X described a culture within her secondary school of high awareness of caste, which has damaging consequences for pupils of lower caste. She also described an incident where a teacher asked her openly what caste she was from, in which she felt humiliated. Although the bullying happened recently, X had not considered complaining to the school, which raises questions

> about the bullying policy and pastoral care of the school concerned. X believes that interest in caste is largely perpetuated by older members of the Hindu and Sikh community, yet the bullying she experienced was by young people. (pp. 70-71)

The above case shows that caste identities are learnt, encouraged and engrained into the minds of a South Asian, especially Indians right from their childhood and thereby impact their self-image as well as their behaviour with the others. Indeed, even in a different socio-economic setting the members whose culture has been infected by the caste virus, take the virus along with them and pass the same to the next generation. Soon the next generation also starts acting the way the previous one did. Hence, if caste was merely an economic issue, it should have vanished in a new economic setting, which it did not.

Here is another case (Case Study 22) of a woman fairly older that the one discussed in the previous case (pp. 95-97):

> X came to the UK 52 years ago when she was ten years old. She is a Buddhist. She has no caste, but in India her father was a shoemaker. The incident X describes happened in the previous year.
>
> Account of caste discrimination experiences X's mother used to go to a day centre. The clientele were predominantly Punjabi, Sikh Jattladies. X had noticed over the years that if a Sikh or a Jatt went to the centre they were made welcome, but that low caste people were not and were taunted.
>
> Last year X was asked to be trustee of the day centre. She explained that she could only go to the centre infrequently, but this was accepted and she agreed. After an absence of three weeks, she went to the centre and, in front of everyone, nearly all of whom were Sikh, a Sikh woman aged 75 or more said they did not want her there. This was because she did not come frequently enough. The discussion deteriorated into an argument... Eventually she swore at X and said 'You Chamars coming here and trying to take over our centres. In India you're almost like

beggars, but when you come here you think you know it all and you want to take over our centres'...

... X spoke to a member of the management board, but their response was 'what can we do?'. A couple of months ago her mother said to the woman that if she did not stop mentioning Chamars and Valmiki, she would be very upset with her, but the woman effectively said 'you cannot do anything'. Her mother stopped going to the centre. People knew her caste because she had lived in the area a long time and initially there were few Indians.

... X does not feel discriminated against because of her caste. However, she described how caste abuse is used verbally and the words still hurt.

Comments by National Institute of Economic and Social Research (NIESR), United Kingdom:

Owing to the language used, this case appears to show caste harassment. (pp. 95-97)

The abovementioned study conducted to confirm the existence of casteism in the United Kingdom concluded the following:

The study has found evidence that caste discrimination and harassment is likely to occur in Britain. Evidence has been found in respect of work and the provision of services. Whilst not ruling out the possibility of caste discrimination in education, no incidents enabling us to conclude that caste discrimination is likely to occur in education were found. However, **evidence was found of caste-related pupil-on-pupil bullying** and that this was likely to be addressed differently (and less adequately) by schools than bullying related to protected strands (p. 65)

The above study by the National Institute of Economic and Social Research (U.K.) clearly points to the fact that given a different socio-economic setting, the cultural values that perpetuate in Indian natives, keep the ill tradition of caste based discrimination alive. The notion of self is not inborn as per Mead (1934), but learned as a person grows up (Metcalf & Rolfe, 2010) when a person learns to view herself in caste terms based on her learnings passed down from the previous generation then she also learns to view others in caste terms as well and treats them differentially.

Conclusion

In the current article we concluded that the problem of caste is not essentially a problem stemming from any religion. Similarly, it could not be established that casteism is either an urban or a characteristically rural phenomenon and it was concluded that the caste divide is widespread across regions whether rural or urban. It was also established that the reason why the caste factor is manipulated by the politicians is not fundamentally the presence of political systems but due to the fact that it is a fault line of which anyone can take advantage. Finally, the debate whether casteism is an economic or a cultural issue was evaluated and it emerged that while it is both an economic as well as a cultural problem, the fundamental solution lies in the change of mind-sets.

An equation that can sum the strategy suggested by the whole article can be represented in the following manner:

'Empowerment of the depressed castes' × 'Culture Change of the advantaged castes' = Holistic Growth

The future generations need to be relieved of the indoctrinations about caste identities whichare prevalent in the nation. A positive identification, not a divisive one will have to ensue to shape progressive mind-sets. As to what or who can change the mind-set of the entire nation, is a question that has an obvious answer – everyone. The teachers, the politicians, the media, the parents, the workers, the professionals, the artists, the bureaucrats and the reader are the ones who can change the culture of the nation by establishing new values based on unity and progress rather than divisiveness and competition.

Up Next...

The next chapter attempts to understand the problem of communalism – another arch-virus infecting the Indian society. The reader should while reading the next chapter, keep notice of how casteism and communalism have much in common and are of course, cousins. The third chapter elucidates further on the nature of casteism, communalism and other such viruses infecting the society and argues that in effect all these viruses belong to the same family of - separatism. It also attempts to explore deeper into the 'how' part of dealing with these problems and attempts to create a framework through which these separatist issues can be dealt with.

Readers can meanwhile take a break and go through the attachment appended at the end of this article, drawing similarities between communal riots and violence and caste based violence captured in form of short caselets. The communal violence stories have not been covered here under the assumption that the reader would have heard enough already, if not experienced, incidences of communal violence(s) in the nation. In case if the reader is still unaware of the communal discord that has been prevalent in the nation, then an exercise of asking around elders, watching some movies on the partition of India, reading 'Freedom at Midnight by Larry Collins and Dominique Lapierre, works by Dr Irfan Habib, Dr Bipan Chandra, and other scholars, could be educative and enlightening.

References

1. TRP = Target Rating Points.
2. Data collected only taking into consideration the top 14 most populous state in terms of scheduled caste population as per the Census (2011). The States include–Uttar Pradesh, West Bengal, Bihar, Tamil Nadu, Andhra Pradesh, Maharashtra, Rajasthan, Madhya Pradesh, Karnataka, Punjab, Odisha, Haryana, Gujarat and Jharkhand (in decreasing order of scheduled caste population).
3. Strong identification with a group, in fact, influences economic trends as well as outcomes as Akerlof and Kranton(2000) (2005) (2010) have shown, ranging from heterogeneity in preferences (Chen & Li, 2009), differences in prices (Ball, Eckel, Grossman, & Zame, 2001) or conforming to detrimental stereotypes (Hoff & Pandey, 2006). This proves the point that it is in fact, the group mindset that affects economic outcomes. However, the debate whether material milieu shapes the culture or culture shapes the material milieu or whether culture impacts economics or economics shapes culture, is an eternal one (Guiso, Sapienza, & Zingales, 2014). However, the author of the present article is of the inclination that culture and economics is a kind of a chicken and egg story, *i.e.* culture impacts economics impacts culture.
4. Case Study 6.

CHAPTER 2

Perspectives on Communalism

Unlike the previous chapter this one takes a historiographical tone. This chapter is a combination of the lectures of Professor Sanjay Verma delivered at Kirori Mal College, University of Delhi in the months of August-September 2010 (when I happened to be a student there) and the assignments submitted to him on the same topic. This was also not long after when the Hon'ble Supreme Court stayed the "Ayodhya Verdict" of the Hon'ble Allahabad High Court (Uttar Pradesh)[1]. It is the longest running legal dispute in India. Call it by any make-up Babri Masjid Dispute or Ram Mandir Dispute, but it simply boils down to just who owns a piece of sixty by fourty square feet of land in Ayodhya, where the Babri Masjid used to stand till December 6, 1992. Babur, the Mughal emperor, is said to have built a mosque on the same premises as that of the said birthplace of Lord Rama. Centuries later this premise became a point of contention among the Hindu and Muslim communalists and was the cause behind much rioting and bloodshed that engulfed the whole nation. The first clash regarding this piece of land took place in 1853 when Wajid Ali Shah was still the Nawab of Awadh. The Allahabad High Court on 30th September 2010 ruled by majority that the disputed land in Ayodhyabe divided into three parts: the site of Lord Rama's idol to be allocated for the temple, the 'SitaRasoi' and 'Ram Chabutra' to Nirmohi Akhara and the rest to the Sunni Wakf Board.In a recent interview[2], IrfanHabib regarding the said dispute rightly commented that "This (dispute) should never have been viewed as an issue between Hindus and Muslims. It was in fact a confrontation between the forces of secularism and humanism on one side and the forces of communalism on the other."

I was nearly three years old when the Babri masjid riots took place in Firozabad. In the limited consciousness I must have possessed at that age, I can still recall with clarity, that all the children in the house including me, were told that 'riots' or 'dange' as we call it in Hindi, have taken place in the city. I and other cousins of my age did not understand the meaning of most of the things at that tender age, but we did understand that something had happened which needed to be feared, which was horrific and dangerous. It is a commonly held story in Firozabad that a person of one community who had given some loan to a person of the other community, would frequent the residence of the borrower to recover his dues. One fine day, in the background of the communal violence that had started from Ayodhya, the borrowers murdered the lender when he asked to repay the arrears and this is how the riots began in the city of Firozabad. Over the years I got a chance to interact with people from both the communities – Hindu and Muslim - in the post-riot Firozabad. They say that the city had transformed into something very different in the rioting days. People of different communities who shared amicable relations would secretly inform their friends of the other community warning them not to come in their area for it would be too dangerous. "But I used to come here everyday" the person would protest and his friend would say "this, my friend is not everyday…hundreds of women are leaving the city by the day with their children, but where will they go?.Youngsters from outside, people whom no one has ever seen before are entering the city to flare violence! This city has gone mad."[3]

Opposing point of views: Who shares the onus?

Communalism is the second of the social viruses we shall be dealing with in this series of essays. The problem of communalism indeed led to the partition of India and still haunts the society with bloody tales of crimes against humanity. In India, communalism is not merely restricted to the Hindu-Muslim conflict, as there have been instances of communal strife in tribal communities of the north-eastern regions of India and among people of other religions other than Hindu and Islam. However, the most prevalent form of communal strife in India is the so called divide between the Hindus and Muslims of this nation.

Over the years a blame game has followed that attempts to scapegoat one community or the other for the problem of communalism in the nation, which again presents the classic case of wrong diagnosis. Perhaps the wrong diagnosis is intentional, as has been argued by many. There are debates regarding the nature and origin of communalism – whether it is an economic or an ideological issue; whether it stems from political or economic interest, or from religion? - Like the problem of casteism, these questions have also emerged in the discussions around the problem of communalism. The contention from the previous chapter is forwarded in this chapter – arguing that communalism, likecasteism is essentially a cultural problem. The difference in communalism and casteism is only that in the latter, many groups fight among each other in scattered battlefields while in the prior, two large groups fight on a larger arena - but the magnitude of harm caused by both the troubles may well be the same.

Before entering the historiographical discussions it would be beneficial to take a look at the debates around the problem of communalism in order to gain a basic clarity on the nature and causes of origins of the communal problem.

A Post-First World War Phenomenon?

There are historians and sociologists who contend that communalism is essentially a post- First World War phenomenon.They argue that amidst the economic depression and delirium that followed after the First World War communalism was a natural response to the post-War environment[4]. They even liken communalism to fascism (which is not a wrong analogy by any means).

However, Professor Zahiruddin Faruki has traced the events of communal riots in India dating back to 1809 when according to his study of the district gazetteer of Benares "Communal riots had taken place wherein the Hindus destroyed about fifty mosques and the Muslims also destroyed a number of temples" (Faruki, 1977). Faruki's argument proves that communalism is not essentially a post-First World War phenomenon.

To say that communalism was absent in India before the First World War would be equivalent to saying that the concept of Aryan dominance in Germany was completely an invention of Hitler and that discrimination against the Jews in Germany was not prevalent before the First World War–both of which would be erroneous arguments. While the World war certainly protracted the divide between communities, it can by no means be argued that a crevice was not already present before the dawn of the War.

Hindus or Muslims?

Muslim Middle Class Assertion or Hindu Revivalism?

According to sociologists like W.C. Smith, the communal conflict was due to the backwardness of the Muslims which had certain historical causations. The reason according to Smith for such backwardness was the "relatively late arrival of the 'Muslim middle class' in the Indian Society". Others have made similar formulations when they have claimed that the Muslim middle class pushed Sir Syed towards a politics of preferential treatment[5]. According to them, it was this weakness in the position of the Muslim middle class that convinced Sir Syed that Muslims were not yet ready to enter into an anti-imperialist struggle. Such formulations, made by Smith and others are the result of interpretations made by W.W. Hunter to outlay the policy of the British after the Revolt of 1857. According to Hunter, the unfavourable conditions (after the Revolt), for the British demanded certain positive action, that would win the support of the Muslims who were relatively backward and thus more likely to get influenced by the British (Hunter, 1872). Professor Verma at this point of time explained – "this backwardness of the Muslims became a given for the social scientists outside India, who were unaware of the Indian conditions".

Another point of view has been taken up by thinkers like Beni Prasad who traces the roots of communalism in the essentially Hindu reform and revival movements. These movements, he argued tried to do away with certain practices such as child marriage and *sati*, by developing an understanding that such practices were essentially inhuman and were not mentioned in the "Holy Books". Hence, the reform revival movements, according to Beni Prasad, attempted to purify the religion on the basis of what it was two thousand years back and "by doing so, the evolution of religion developed in the past thousand years became meaningless" (Prasad, 1946) . According to Prasad, this also resulted in the separation of religions on the basis of their past – one went to Vedic and Puranic scriptures and the other to Persian and Arabic texts – which reflected absolutely different geographies, culture and language. The symbols which had evolved over a long period of coexistence and were reminiscent of a composite culture, explains Prasad, thus, became meaningless. Many have thus argued that it was only after Dayanand Saraswati, that the cow became an issue of conflict.

Hindu Identity or Islam?

The argument that the Turkish advent or the so called Muslim Rule in India was primarily the starting point of communalism also seems erroneous. According to James Jones, Ashoka, the Great Indian Emperor (304-232 BCE) is said to have ordered killings of 18,000 Jains after someone drew a picture of Buddha bowing at the feet of Mahavira; which points to the argument that Communalism in India is not necessarily a result of the coming of the Turks but has existed from before (Jones, 2008). Eminent historians such as Satish Chandra, Irfan Habib, and Firdos Anwar have extensively argued that the Turkish invasion, the Sultanate(s) and the Mughal rule in India were never essentially anti-Hindus and were simply political dominions of dynasties rather than dictatorships of religious groups. In fact, in most of the aforementioned realms, Hindus had formed a considerable proportion of the nobility and the ruling elite and religion never became a prime consideration in statecraft (Anwar, 2001).

Communalism is represented on ideological lines by the Hindu and Muslim communalists of the 1920s and 1930s. A monograph called 'Hindutva' that was published by V.D. Savarkar appealed to the slogan of "Hindi-Hindu-Hindustan". *i.e.* the country belongs exclusively to the Hindus. This monograph has presented Muslims as "foreign invaders who had ruled over the Hindus for centuries with utter cruelty" (Savarkar). Also, it assumes the monolithic origins of the Hindu and the Muslim religion. A counterpart of this philosophy was Muslim extremism which had raised the slogan of "Islam in danger"!

Both sets of arguments, on whether communalism was born out of moderate Hindu aspirations or moderate Muslim aspirations (dealt in the section Muslim Middle Class Assertion or Hindu Revivalism?) or whether it was born out of extreme Hinduism or extreme Islam (dealt in the section Hindu Identity or Islam?) are erroneous. The fact is whether moderate or extreme, the onus, in final analysis cannot be laid on one particular community or the other, as members of both the communities point fingers towards each other without conclusively putting the onus on the real issue – that is:

a. Either ideological weakness on part of all citizens of the nation[6],
b. Or personal political or economic interest in an environment of scarcity and over population
c. Or both

The arguments of non-right wing thinkers run counter to the thought of Hindu and Muslim communalists. According to them there is no such religion that originally existed with the name 'Hinduism'. There were various levels of identities such as cultural, geographical, ethnic etc. and generally a single person possesses these multiple identities at the same time. Romila Thapar, for example, argues that the assumption of monolithic origins of the so called Hinduism is a myth. She calls it the "Tyranny of labels" (Thapar, 1996).

It was, according to many historians, the attempt of the right wing groups and the British colonialist government to present the Indian history in communal terms, for example by marking periods of Indian history in communal language—The Ancient Indian history classified as the era of Hindu rule, The Medieval history as the era of Muslim rule (Chandra S., 2003). It is due to such erroneous classifications, modern historians have sought more secular and indeed logical periodisation(s). B.D. Chattopadhyay, for example has argued that there was indeed a medieval era in India much before the Muslims or Turks arrived in the Indian Subcontinent in his book 'The Making of Early Medieval India' (Chattopadhyaya, 1994) thereby taking a step towards periodisation of history in terms of historical development rather than in religious terminology. Hence, Hinduism is not concomitant to Ancient India and Islam is not concomitant to Medievalism.

Historiographical Discussion

Generally, studies on the subject of communalism era can be divided into two broad categories (apart from the ones mentioned above): (i) The Primordialists, and (ii) The Instrumentalists.[7] While the historiography of the British Raj or the colonial historians seems closer to the primordial point of view, the Nationalist and Marxist historians seem to be more in favour of the Instrumentalist line of thought. In premordialism, it is believed that the various communities in the society are fundamentally different and the awareness regarding this is cultivated from birth itself "Ever since birth, one is reminded of his religion, through observation of rituals and rites *(from the cradle to the grave)*". The premordialists hold that the religious identity and moreover the level of religiosity that exists in India is the primary cause of communalism.

The instrumentalists on the other hand have a different understanding of communalism. According to this interpretation, communalists or certain minority of people with political ambitions use the differences among the majority of the people to serve and further their own interest. Thus, according to the instrumentalists, the conflict is about something other than religion. There are personal vested interests of individuals or groups that create differences under the garb of religion. Hence, communalism, according to the instrumentalists is a tool to perpetuate personal interest. K.M. Ashraf puts this aspect in an appropriate phrase when he describes communalism as *"Mazhab ki siyasi dukandari"*[8].

A third line of thought that positions itself somewhere between the primordial and the nationalist thought has been taken up by Bipan Chandra and has been further argued in the next chapter. According to this line of thought, there are essentially no fundamental differences in any two groups that position themselves against each other; nor does religiosity has a major role to play in such a positioning, but it is basically a certain form of group based ideologies of the human beings that leads them to identify with their own group and ostracize the other under the influence of personal interests and the perception that interests of the other group are antithetical to the interest of one's own group.

All these three lines of thoughts shall be discussed in this essay one by one.

The communal virus being one of the most potent, comparatively recent and most visible of the viruses infecting the nation was used as a tool to subjugate the country under colonial dominance. Keeping this virus alive or eradicating the same became the primary contention between the British Raj and the Nationalists during the Indian National Movement.While the colonialists attempted to spread the virus, the Nationalists endeavoured to contain it and exterminate it. In the pursuit of a political tussle between the colonialists and the nationalists, the communal issue led these two competing groups to define the very essence of the Indian society in fairly different and divergent terms. Gyanendra Pandey has argued that communalism was a term coined by the British officials and had not gained currency until the late 19th century. He further adds that the Nationalists accepted and popularised the use of such a terminology in their writings (to counter the Right wing movements within the country and the 'British Divide and Rule' policy). However, - both the writings (of nationalists and colonialists) show essentialism; while the colonialists are essentially racialists, the nationalists are essentially rationalists – *i.e.* the colonialists essentially stress on the inherent disunity of India while the nationalists stress on the inherent unity in India that always existed (Pandey, 2012).

It would be worthwhile to take a brief look at the colonial or the British Imperialist understanding of the communal issue and thereafter a detailed view of the nationalist understanding before touching upon any other interpretations on the subject of communalism and the Indian identity.

I British Imperialist Perception

The British colonisers were of the belief that the Indian subcontinent is populated by nationalities that were, since time immemorial, in conflict with each other. Especially ever since the advent of Islam in India, Hindus and Muslims have lived under constant hostility. With this assumption in mind, the British had always interpreted Indian history as one suffering from communal disharmony and social discord. India was seen not as a composite whole but as a geographical expression, comprising of disunited groups. Winston Churchill once remarked in the same breath that "India is merely a geographical expression. It is no more a single country than the Equator."

According to the colonialists, there was no common thread, no common characteristic, which bound the whole Indian nation together. For them India was an arbitrary term given to a group of people who had perhaps been under the hegemony of a single ruler for some arbitrary reason. The puzzle of India was baffling and at the same time enticing, mesmerising for the colonialists. Indeed, their idea of a nation and the feeling of nationalism were closely linked to their experience of history in Europe. Germany was perhaps to them a prime and recent example of a nation formed on the basis of a common language, America was a nation because it had been founded by a set of enterprising Europeans who had racial and/or cultural commonalities. On the other hand, India was viewed as a paradox since neither race, nor religion, nor topography, not even a language or culture bound this country together into a single thread and hence this place was seen as a competing ground for different nationalities and disparate interests groups.

In the absence of nationalism, the characteristic feature of India to the colonialists was communalism. However, a gradual shift in the

Imperial understanding of communalism can be noted from 1890s to 1931 on the basis of official records of the times opines Gyanendra Pandey. This period shows a gradual acceptance of nationalism in the Indian socio-political scenario, however, communalism was still seen as a dominant factor characterising the Indian society. The reductionist tendencies of the colonialist discourse made it appear as if the disturbances were part of a continuum of Indian society and, thus, provided justification for colonial rule and Gyanendra Pandey establishes how the British created a "master narrative" of communalism to understand sectarian strife and the Indian reality.

However, the British colonial interpretation of India is mistaken because communalism is not merely a characteristic feature of the Indian society; it is not limited to geographies. The crusades of medieval Europe were nothing but communalism, but it does not suggest that the whole continuum of European history is based on communal lines. Communal strife has also been seen in the 1994 Rwanda genocide. Just like it would be wrong to characterise all European or African history in fundamentally communal terms, it would also be wrong to characterise India in the same manner as well.

II Indian Nationalist Understanding

The nationalist historiography on the other hand, runs counter to the arguments formulated by the imperialist scholars. According to nationalist scholars, the Hindu-Muslim relationship in the pre-colonial era should be characterised as one of mutual harmony and coexistence.

Communalism earlier was perhaps accepted as a general tendency and uniform and unilateral phenomenon. However, during the course of the Indian National Movement, this perception changed as the idea of "unity in diversity" developed and the Indian history began to be seen in these perspectives. Moreover, a serious attempt was made to understand how this "coexistence in plurality" was maintained in the past by examining policies like Ashoka's Dhamma and Akbar's Sulh-i-kul. However, what came in this period as the most serious departure in the nationalist understanding of communalism was the realisation and identification of the British policy of "Divide and Rule".

The fact that there was indeed a common thread that bound India together is represented in the point that three key personalities: one who claimed himself to be a Hindu, the other an atheist and the third a Muslim and all three belonging to different regions, **still had a common notion of the Indian identity.** The commonly held views of these three demographically disparate personalities stand testimony to the fact that there was something that bound the Indian nation together. Gaining an insight into the views of these three personalities—Jawaharlal Nehru, Maulana Abdul Kalam Azad and Mahatma Gandhi—would be most beneficial for the understanding of the identity of India as well as the communal problem.

Jawaharlal Nehru

Perhaps it was Jawaharlal Nehru who came up for the first time with a structured approach in understanding communalism. He writes in his 'Discovery of India' that "the communal problem, as it was called, was one of adjusting the claims of the minorities and giving them sufficient protection from majority action". He added that "Minorities in India, it must be remembered, are not racial or national minorities as in Europe, they are religious minorities". He then writes "Latterly, religion in any real sense of the word has played little part in Indian political conflicts, though often the word is used and exploited… In political matters, religion is displaced by what is called communalism, a narrow group mentally basing itself on a religious community but in reality concerned with political power and patronage for the interested groups…"

It was this "vested interest of the natives" that according to Nehru created a "triangle, with the government in a position to play off one side against the other by giving special privileges." These special privileges according to Nehru remained confined to "petty appointments in the subordinate public services" and "instead of raising all round standards merit was often sacrificed."

According to Nehru, the major problem was an economic one "which had nothing to do with a person's religion." He writes, "Class conflicts there might well be, but not religious conflicts, except in so far as religion itself presented some vested interests."

In fact, according to Nehru, "the whole history of India was witness of the toleration of minorities and even encouragement of different racial groups." He adds, "There is nothing in the Indian history to compare with the bitter feuds and persecutions that prevailed in Europe… So we did not have to go abroad for ideas of religious and cultural toleration; these were inherent in Indian life." However as per Nehru, a political barrier was created by the British reversing the unifying and amalgamating process which had been going on for centuries, and which was inevitably speeded up by technological developments. According to Nehru there was "some canker that corrupted the entire system". The ideology perpetrated by the colonialists created a situation wherein with time, "people had grown so accustomed to think along communal lines of religious cleavage, and were continually being encouraged to do so by communal religious organisations and government action that the fear of the major religious community, that is the Hindus, swamping others continued to exercise the minds of many Moslems. In the Moslem majority provinces the problem was reversed, for there protection was demanded by the other minority groups (such as Hindu and Sikh) as against the Moslem majority."

With regards to communal organisations, Nehru wrote that "there was a far greater tendency for careerists and opportunists to enter." Regarding their ways he commented that he had made a close study of Nazi methods of propaganda since Hitler's rise to power and…"was astonished to find something very similar taking place in India." According to Nehru, the communal organisations whether Hindu or Muslim, were closely associated to the feudal and conservative elements and were opposed to any revolutionary change[9]. Thus, the "…real conflict had, therefore, nothing to do with religion, but was essentially between those who stood for a nationalist democratic-socially revolutionary policy and those who were concerned with preserving the relics of a feudal regime. In a crisis, the latter inevitably depended on foreign support which is interested in maintaining a status quo."

Hence, according to Nehru, the communal problem was not a temporary evil which tended to fade away with the developing political consciousness. Rather the solution rested in "**a forward educational policy** and **a definitive program to alleviate poverty and unemployment** for the economically and educationally backward groups of the society" (Nehru, 1946).

Maulana Azad

Maulana Abdul Kalam Azad, one of the most acknowledged scholars of his times shared similar views as that of Nehru. In his autobiography 'India Wins Freedom' he wrote that "The real problems of the country were economic, not communal. The differences related to classes, not to groups. He further added that "it is perhaps the greatest frauds on people to suggest that religious affinity can unite those who are geographically, economically, linguistically and culturally different" pointing towards the creation of the separate nation of Pakistan comprising of the two East and West portions of the Indian sub-continent. According to him, "partition would only create disunity in the country, that comprised the British agenda"(Azad).

Mahatma Gandhi

Gandhi's conception of communalism changed with time. In his earliest writing on communalism before the World War I, he considered communalism to be a religious matter that could be solved through religion. "It is easy enough to be friendly to one's friends but to be friend the one who regards himself as your enemy is the quintessence of true religion. The other is mere business..."[10] said Gandhi encouraging his followers to subside communal hatred by giving a religious appeal. In fact, Gandhi was perhaps the first person to have understood the solution to the communal problem when in 1920 he wrote that the solution "consists in our having a common purpose, a common goal and common sorrows. It is best promoted by co-operating to reach the same goal by sharing one another's sorrows and by mutual toleration."[11]

However, after the communal riots following the Non-Cooperation movement, his understanding of communalism went through a definitive shift – from communalism being a religious problem, it was now seen as a social problem which could only be solved by "inter-dining and inter-marriage".

Later around 1931 in the post-depression period, there was yet another shift in his understanding of communalism, in the wake of economic aspects that had emerged markedly across the globe. Gandhi realised that Communalism was not only a social problem but a "socio-economic" one which could only be solved by reducing the socio-economic imbalances in the country.

Finally, in the later years of the British Raj Gandhi expressed his views on communalism in terms of the divide and rule policy of the British: "They can retain their hold on India only by a policy of divide and rule. A living unity between Hindus and Muslims is fraught with danger to their rule. It would mean an end to it."[12]

One would notice that the 3C's formula furnished in the next chapter as a way out of the separatist problem, which has emerged as the basis of the study of researches conducted over many years, was in essence identified by Mahatma Gandhi at a much earlier time. Though the solution came to him in phases, when he wove it together, he led a nation towards independence and freedom.

III Marxist Understanding

The Marxist perspective tries to provide an ideological alternative to the nationalist understanding as well as the British or Imperial understanding. Marxist writings try to explain communalism in class terms – "A pre-industrial colonial society was experiencing peasant radicalisation. At times, the peasantry was dominantly Muslim and at times vice-versa", explains Dr R.P. Dutt. According to him, the situation in the urban centres was similar to that of the villages where there were economic imbalances rather than religious. These were the disparities, as per Dutt, which are characteristic of a proto-capitalist society and have nothing to do with religious differences (Dutt).

A.R. Desai, on similar lines has explained that "in Bengal, the landlords and moneylenders are Hindus and peasants are Muslims, the same is the case in Punjab. In Aligarh and Bulandshahr region, it is just the opposite, while in Malabar, the urban elite were Hindus and the poor artisans Muslims" (Desai).

Thus, the political and economic clashes of different communities were given a communal form by communalists. The various struggles were classified by K.B. Krishna in his book 'The Problem of Minorities', as follows[13]:

1. There is class struggle between the professional classes of different communities and faiths.
2. The struggle is also spread the commercial, industrial and shop keeping trading classes of different faiths and communities.
3. Lastly, there are struggles between the conservative classes of different faith arising from backwardness, illiteracy, mechanisations of rival politicians, mob frenzy and all the social contradictions of the society.

"These struggles arising from the social economy of the country, are accelerated in an epoch of the development of Indian Capitalism under feudal conditions; by British Imperialism; by its policy of counterpoise" concluded Krishna(1939).

IV The Ideological/Inter-group Conflict Explanation

Bipan Chandra, in his later writings has considered communalism to be an ideology. He writes that "communalism starts with the belief that in India, people be organised, grouped together, for secular (that is economic, political, social and cultural) purposes, around their religious identities." "This belief is the starting point of communalism" he writes, "but is not communalism as such." According to him communalism or communal ideology has three basic elements or stages, one following the other:

Stage 1 (Liberal): First, it is the belief that people who follow the same religion have common secular interests, that is, common political, economic, social and cultural interests.

> **Stage 2 (Moderate):** The second element rests on the notion that the secular interests of the followers of one religion are dissimilar and divergent from the interests of the followers of another religion.
>
> **Stage 3 (Extreme):** The stage of extreme communalism is reached when the interests of the followers of different religions and different 'communities' are seen as mutually incompatible, antagonistic and hostile.
>
> Bipan Chandra adds that—
>
> ... though these stages of communalism were different from one another, they also interacted and provided a certain continuum. One stage fed the other and thus liberal communalist found it difficult to prevent ideological transition to extreme communalism (as was the case with M.A. Jinnah).

Moreover, he argues that communalism must also be seen as a single ideology that takes different forms. "Hindu, Sikh, Muslim and Christian communalisms are variants of the same communal ideology".(Chandra B., 1989). He adds that "different communalisms oppose each other only on the surface. In reality, they do not negate each other, they support each other, they feed on each other." Bipan Chandra views the failure of the National Movement in eradicating communal tensions, in terms of their inability to fight communalism on an ideological level. He writes in his article "Communalism: The Way Out" that the solution for the communal problem is the separation of religion from politics and waging a political and ideological struggle against communalism and also by making serious efforts to settle the communal question through compromises and conciliation, by looking for 'soft options'.

This point of view is different from the premordialist and instrumentalist point of view. It is different from the premordialist view because unlike premordialism it does not blame religiosity of identification with a group as the cause of communalism. Rather it argues that the reductionist tendencies with reference to identities that come as a result of group formations and the *"perception" of fundamental distinctness and opposition* of one's own group vis-à-vis the other group creates conflict. Similarly, this point of view is also not totally in line with the instrumentalist one as it does not posit a conspiracy theory in essence. While it does argue that the "perception" of a common interest in one's own group and the "perception" of antithetical interests of the other groups create conflicts, it does not put the complete onus of the conflict over a group of people who create such a separatist mind-set, it accepts a degree of separatism that grows on people because of strong group identities and then this already present degree of separatism is taken advantage of by people for perpetuating their own political interests.

In the next chapter it is explained and argued that essentially communalism, casteism and other such issues are essentially inter-group conflicts. The solutions to the problem of communalism and its close cousins – casteism, regionalism etc. have also been discussed in the next essay in detail taking forward the point of view discussed in this section.

Conclusion

While there is much debate on whether communalism is inherent to the Indian society or has been a result of the coming of various peoples who came and settled in this land, or whether it is a result of political ambition (British or Indian), what is true is that the problem of communalism is a dangerous fault line in the Indian social fabric. According to me no society in history whether at one point of time in the history or at another seems devoid of fault lines. The crusades in Europe, racial conflicts in the United States of America, the Shia-Sunni conflict in the Middle-East, the tribal conflicts in Africa, the linguistic conflicts in China and a variety or combinations of all such conflicts present across the globe, are nothing but different genres of separatism at play. At the base of these separatist conflicts are two levers – first being self-interest and the second being a tendency to put single labels of identities on groups wherein members may have multiple identities in reality. As long as these two levers are not identified by people, and as long as the realisation does not come that the seemingly beneficial outcomes of separatist politics are in reality more detrimental than beneficial in the long run, sustainable progress for people will remain an impossibility. Yet positive examples set by some parts of Europe, and even parts of India (which are larger in size and population than any country or region in Europe), can serve as an inspiration and aspiration for establishing social harmony in other regions as well.These regions have shown that the dissipation of fault lines is possible. Indeed new fault lines, of different natures, do emerge from time to time in these regions[14]; however, perhaps the knowledge of past experiences leads these peoples to make amends in order to suppress these fault lines and such tacit knowledge is reflected in the policies and civic bodies that these regions form, the culture of symbiosis which is reflected indeed in the socio-economic growth of these regions.

The following chapter takes into consideration the views discussed in this brief historiographical attempt and those discussed in the previous chapter (at times supporting the views and at times refuting them) to discuss communalism, casteism and even regionalism etc. as variants of separatisms. The next chapter categorises these fault lines as basically inter-group conflicts. Some of the viewpoints present in this article and the previous one are also taken into consideration to come up with a synthesis of a "way out" to the problem of separatism in the country.

References

1. In an assignment I submitted to Professor Verma in September 2010, I had scribbled a note in the conclusion which said *"the kind of safety measures employed by the government by stationing large number of para-military and police forces in various districts (on the day of the verdict) is a clear signifier that the communal threat still looms over India and haunts the mind of an Indian"*.To which Professor Verma after one of the classes told me in the corridor *"Your conclusion in the essay is correct"* and we had a long discussion on the subject post that.
2. http://articles.economictimes.indiatimes.com/2014-12-07/news/56802785_1_secular-forces-communal-forces-aligarh-muslim-university.
3. The same friends when reunited after the riots would narrate this dialogue to me years later.
4. Tasca highlights the psychological role played by the war-caused "excitement" and "delirium" that made the public more susceptible to extreme radicalism [see: Felice, Renzo de, The Interpretations of Fascism (Le interpretazioni del fascismo),1995.]

5. These views are similar to the explanations of the rise of Fascism provided by commentators such as Denis Mack Smith, Edmond Vermeil, William M. McGovern, Peter Viereck and others, who have argued that fascism was the result of the historical development of certain countries (like Germany and Italy). The middle class in these countries was late in arrival and therefore was weak and dependent. Thus, it took the support of illiberal, anti-democratic and conservative alliances, which crystallised into Fascism and Nazism. Also, these countries had developed features like militarism, anti-Semitism, authoritarianism etc. during their struggle for national unification. These factors combined, gave birth to fascism.
6. In similar observation Historians like Benedetto Croce, FreidrichMeinecke, Gerhard Ritter, Hans Kohn and Golo Mann have perceived fascism as the result of "Europe's moral disease".
7. In relation to fascism a similar debate has been documented by Renzo de Felice in his book, "Interpretations of Fascism". This debate is between the 'intentionalists' and 'structuralists'. The 'intentionalists' stress the role of political ambition in the creation of fascist regimes but the 'structuralists' to see these regimes as the products of powerful ideological, social and economic institutional forces interacting within the contexts of the new dictatorships. The 'structuralists' in the Indian debate are the 'premordialists' and the 'intentionalists' are the 'instrumentalists'.
8. Ashraf, K.M. (1959), Hindustani Muslim Siyasat Par Ek Nazar, Bombay, 1959 reprint in Urdu.
9. A similar view is held by Barrington Moore Jr. regarding Fascism. Barrington Moore Jr. observed that fascism is one of either three or four avenues leading from pre-industrial society to modern society. This road to modernisation is the capitalist-reactionary way, along which the moderate-conservative-agrarian attempt was made to counter impending industrialisation and massification with a "revolution from above".
10. U R Rao, ed. The Way to Communal Harmony, by M.K. Gandhi, Navajivan Publishing House Ahamedabad, 1994, p.12.
11. M K Gandhi, Young India, 25-2-1920, p. 3.
12. M K Gandhi, Harijan, 4-5-1940, p. 315.
13. Richard Lowenthal in a similar tone related the rise of fascism to the changes in the class structure of the society caused by the crisis provoked by WWI. These changes are –
    (1) A proportional increase in the non-productive sectors of the population – permanently unemployed, property holders, workers in distribution systems, and administrations.
    (2) Social mobility within the working class – decrease in the number of specialized labourers, coupled with an increase in their indispensability; and development of a new class of technicians.
    (3) An economic wasting away of small producers.

One of the consequences of these changes was the creation of new interest groups, which led to the creation of a basic conflict within the ranks of middle class, proletariat and the bourgeoisie.

14. Proactive use of such learning could be beneficial in the north-eastern region of India. While helping Dr Rekha Dwivedi (Research Director at National Foundation for Communal Harmony), in editing articles written by 'Group A' Civil Servants of India, I observed that many articles I edited stressed on the impeding dangers of growing communalism in the north-eastern tribes of the nation.

CHAPTER 3

Separatism it is! (Nature and Solutions)

In this article an attempt is made to understand the concept of casteism and communalism as a subset or as a manifestation of the broader concept of separatism. Separatism in turn has been understood as an ideology that emanates from two basic tendencies: (i) to form groups and reduce self-and others' identities to a single label; and (ii) in ascribing unique interests to identity groups (or labels)–interests that are unique for a group, divergent and even opposed to that of other groups. The consequence of separatism is inter-group conflict argues this essay. A framework is then traced to demonstrate how the separatist mind-set grows in a society and takes a self-sustaining form. Then a brief attempt is made to delineate the historical growth of casteism and communalism in line with the framework that is laid in the article - of the growth of the separatist mind-set. Finally, solutions to inter-group conflict with the view of finding solutions to the problem of separatism in India are explored.

Introduction to the concept of Separatism

Just as the Indian democracy stands on the four pillars of the Legislature, the Judiciary, the Executive and now, considered by many – a free Press; the democracy also suffers threats by the four divisive axes of conflict as pointed out by a modern historian (Guha, 2007)– those of Caste, Language, Religion and Class. These conflict axes have been cause of most of the riots, atrocities and political manoeuvring in the nation. All these conflicts are essentially identity oriented, culturally perpetuated, inter-group conflicts. All these axes are in essence 'separatist' ambitions in one form or the other.

The divisive forces of Caste and Religion are perhaps the oldest and the most enduring ones in the Indian context. There has been much debate around the fact that whether the problem of caste and religion in India is actually an economic issue with cultural implications or a cultural issue with economic implications. It will be attempted in this article to prove the latter by showing that not only economic differences, but any kind of differences can lead people to identify themselves into groups and that the groups, feeding on separatist ideologies become antagonistic to each other resulting into the creation of a situation of social strife.

Separatist Ideology - the Cause of Communalism and Casteism

In this article it is contended that the separatist ideology uses the group behaviour and identity formation as strategic tools to inject itself into the culture of the masses.

All major conflicts in this world are essentially 'inter-group' conflicts. It is in fact, in the very nature of the human beings to form groups, identify themselves with groups and differentiate as well as discriminate between themselves and the members of other groups. Studies in the psychology of group behaviour such as those undertaken by Tajfel et al. (1971); Chen and Li (2009), show that individuals exhibit strong in-group preferences and reluctance towards members of other groups, even when groups are formed arbitrarily.

Such studies show that people behave in irrational manners to confirm to group opinions even when the groups are formed arbitrarily – with no actual common factor. Given the arbitrary nature of group formation, it is difficult to ascertain whether a particular case of discrimination against a group is due to economic, political, cultural or ideological factors. It may very well be possible that the fundamental idea, around which the group would have originally formed, may not play a part and may not be the cause in the later discriminatory mind-set of the group. All that we know is that members of a group condition themselves and their next generations to behave in certain manners and perceive the world in a certain way based on commonly held ideas, beliefs, biases, assumptions and perceptions handed down in forms of symbols and ideas[1].

Such studies show that people behave in irrational manners to confirm to group opinions even when the groups are formed arbitrarily–with no actual common factor. These studies rest on a theoretical construct used by psychologists to explain irrational individual behaviour of human beings in a group scenario. The concept is known as – 'Groupthink'. Groupthink is a psychological phenomenon that occurs within a group of people, in which the desire for harmony or conformity in the group results in an irrational or dysfunctional decision-making outcome (Turner & Pratkanis, 1998). Turner and Pratkanis explain that:

> Loyalty to the group requires individuals to avoid raising controversial issues or alternative solutions, and there is loss of individual creativity, uniqueness and independent thinking. The dysfunctional group dynamics of the 'ingroup,' produces an 'illusion of invulnerability' (an inflated certainty that the right decision has been made). Thus, the 'ingroup' significantly overrates its own abilities in decision-making, and significantly underrates the abilities of its opponents (the 'outgroup'). Furthermore groupthink can produce dehumanising actions against the 'outgroup'.

Group think does not only operate on the organisational level but also on a much larger level – i.e. the level of formation of the social structure. Dehumanising actions against the 'outgroup(s)' has been a phenomenon that can be traced in the annals of history as well as in the contemporary world across regions. Across time and space, human beings have formed groups and have stigmatised those not belonging to their own group. Often they have indulged in excesses of inhuman brutality towards the other groups owing to the irrationality created by the 'Groupthink' phenomenon. The Helots of Greece, the Burakumin untouchables in Japan, the Cagots in Europe (France), the Al-Akhdam in Yemen, the apartheid stricken Africans or the Shudras of India, all have been on the receiving end of the group alienation tendency of the human being. The Nazi holocaust, the Rwanda genocide, the Red Terror in Ethiopia, the Hindu-Muslim riots of Bombay, Godhara, Belchi, Muzaffarnagar and many more are all examples of the separatist mentality and a 'culture of separatism' at playperpetuated by the groupthink tendency and causing inter-group conflicts. Such a mentality has led to pervasive social injustices resulting in widespread loss of life, property and dignity.

How the Separatist Mind-set Grows–A Framework

The renowned Indian Historian Bipan Chandra provided a framework to illustrate the growth and spread of communal ideology in India. He has tracked a trend in the antagonisms between the Hindu and Muslims groups in India classifying the mind-set of communal antagonisms along three stages (Chandra, 1989) –

Stage 1: First, it is the belief that people who follow the same religion have common secular interests, that is, common political, economic, social and cultural interests

Stage 2: The second element rests on the notion that the secular interests of the followers of one religion are dissimilar and divergent from the interests of the followers of another religion

Stage 3: The stage of extreme communalism is reached when the interests of the followers of different religions and different 'communities' are seen as mutually incompatible, antagonistic and hostile

The framework furnished by Bipan Chandra can be used to classify the degree to which the separatist mind-set fuelled by self-interest and groupthink progresses, spreads and becomes self-sustaining.

This has also been reflected in Tajfel's experiments. In this experiment boys who even knew each other from before were randomly divided into groups on the basis of the estimated position of dots by each individual. The dots were shown to them on a screenand they were made to believe that the experimenter was examining visual judgments; the resulting groups were categorised as 'dot-over-estimators' and 'dot-under-estimators'. The boys were given tokens indicating money and were given three alternatives:

a. Make an in-group choice, give both tokens of money to two people who belonged to their own group

b. Make an Out-group choice, give both tokens of money to two people who belonged to the other group

c. Make an Intergroup choice, give one token to a member of own group and one to that of the other group

Most boys chose a ticket which would give their own group the most. Thus, even though there was no sense of hostility or competition between members of two groups earlier, a sort of competitiveness crept in by the mere realisation of belongingness to a particular group. This naturally happens when it is perceived that belonging to a group means common interest in all spheres, which comes with the perception of antithetical interests of the other group.

We can thus come up with a framework using the above theories as our base to map the various degrees of separatist mind-sets. We can combine Tajfel's theory of group behaviour and Bipan Chandra's three stages of communalism to come up with a general theory of separatism that proceeds in four stages.

The stage-wise progression of the same looks something like this:—

Stage 0 (No Separatism): No central idea of group formation

Stage 1: (Liberal Separatism): Emergence of a central idea along which a group is formed coupled with the illusion of commonality in all spheres of life (even the spheres are unrelated to the original idea)

Stage 2 (Moderate Separatism): Realisation that the group is distinct in all spheres of life and other groups are distinct in every sense and in their interests

Stage 3 (Extreme Separatism): Realisation that the interests and the way of life of other groups are antithetical to those of own group.

The separatist mind-set seems to emanate as a strategy aimed at maintaining a *status quo* or propagating a particular group ethos or both in a society. At first, a group is formed along a central idea that creates a feeling of commonality among the people. The group behaviour then takes over in tandem with separatist ambitions to bring together the group and create an illusion of commonality in all spheres of life. Eventually, with the realisation that the way of life of the other group is separate and antithetical to their own group, people start harbouring notions of unhealthy competition and animosity towards the members of the other group.

In fact, human beings can rally around any idea and turn into separatists at the behest of a minority's ambitions, whether it be a genocide or the world war, a football riot or labour violence - all are forms of separatism at play stoked by a flare of marketing. For example, let us consider a situation wherein a marketing manager of an automobile manufacturing firm has been charged with creating an 'animalistic-fundamental loyalty' towards their new automobile being launched in the market called, let's say– the DFG5. Now what the market manager does is to position the automobile in such a way that the users of the DFG5 start seeing themselves as having more things in common than just owning a DFG5. For example, they start seeing themselves as belonging to a particular economic segment, players of a particular sport, as having similar personality traits and as bearers of some common values. Having achieved this, or perhaps having chosen the segment in a manner that the car is actually targeted for the people mentioned above, the marketing manager now wishes to escalate the brand loyalty further. He now by means of marketing creates first the awareness that there are users of a different brand of automobile who belong to a different economic segment than those using the DFG5 and play different sports, have certain common personality traits not similar to those using the DFG5 group and eventually the two groups have very different values. Having achieved this stage, the marketing manager becomes successful at creating the illusion that the users of the DFG5 and the users of some other particular brand of automobiles actually stand for fundamentally different things in life that are antithetical to each other and thus the interests of the users of the DFG5 and those of the users of that other brand are antithetical in all spheres of life. Now, the marketing manager has created a self-sustaining brand loyalty for his brand benefiting out of the inter-group behaviour of the human being. While the users of the automobiles forget that the basic purpose of the vehicle is transportation!

Though the example given above is imaginary (aimed at a theoretical exercise, not necessarily a representation of the reality) and there was no intent on part of the writer to show marketing managers and automobile brands in a demonic light, yet consider such a group-behaviour at play in other contexts that are not dangerous for the society–such as loyalty to a band or to a sports team – and then in contexts that are dangerous, such as caste, class, religion and region.

Historical development of Caste based separatism in India

The caste based separatism in India follows the same line of development resulting into the creation of a stigmatised ethnic identity. The caste system in India was historically formed at a stage where the society reached a level of division of labour to an extent where the professional identity became so strong that it cemented a basis for group identification, which eventually led to the formation of castes in the Indian society. The various 'caste groups' came to believe that they have common extra-economic characteristics. Then the realisation came into being that economic as well as extra-economic characteristics and interests of the other castes were respectively unique and considerably different from those of their own caste. Finally, a belief emerged that everything that the people belonging to another caste stand for, is antithetical to people of their own caste - thereby triggering bitter caste based battles in the entire nation and the original idea that was perhaps a convenient economic arrangement at the time of inception, based on the principles of the division of labour and allowing much socio-economic mobility at that time, eventually became a divisive force in the society. It would be worth understanding this historical progression in detail.

Stage 1: *Emergence of a central idea along which a group is formed coupled with the illusion of commonality in all spheres of life (even the spheres unrelated to the original idea)*

The conflict of caste and class were one and the same for a long period in Indian history when caste was the prime signifier of one's occupational class. It appears that the during the Early Vedic period (1900 to 1500 BC) a nascent form of social stratification based on occupation began to emerge. "Gradually the tribal society was divided into three occupational groups, warriors, priests and the common people on the same pattern as Iran. The fourth division called the 'shudras' appeared towards the end of the Rig Vedic period. The term shudra is mentioned for the first time in the Rig Veda in its tenth book, which is the latest addition" (Sharma R. S., 2005).

However, we may also observe that at the time of the early Vedic period, the concept of being 'born in a caste' had still not taken place and there was much occupational as well as social mobility. Consider, for example, the below paragraph taken from the Rig Veda that shows how in a family, there could be people practicing different occupations:

> "I am a poet, my father is a physician, and my mother is a grinder. Earning a livelihood through different means we live together... "
>
> — Rig Veda, 9.112.3

Stage 2: *Realisation that the group is distinct in all spheres of life and other groups exist that are distinct in every sense and in their interests*

Towards the later Vedic period (1500 to 1000 BC) the society came to be divided on a more stringent order of the 'varna'. Now a person was born into a varna, his occupation being defined at the time of birth itself. Many historians relate this trend with the growth of sedentary lifestyle in the later Vedic society and the production of surplus (Thapar, 2003).

Thus, at this stage while the distribution of surplus was an issue of various group interests, these groups also extended their association and bolstered their respective identities by coming to believe that all, not merely economic, interests of all the members of a particular group are essentially the same. Now a person was 'born in a caste'.

Stage 3: Realisation that the interests and the way of life of other groups are antithetical to those of own group

Once a person was 'born in a caste' it restricted occupational mobility; inter-caste marriage was now not allowed and an overall feeling of competition against other castes in matters of surplus appropriation and politics became acute.

From the later Vedic period onwards we also find the group theories discussed earlier, at work. R.S. Sharma explains that the "later Vedic texts draw a line of demarcation between the three higher orders, on the one hand, and the Shudras on the other" (2005, pp. 124-125). Further, in a text of the later Vedic period "the worst position is reserved for the shudra. He is called the servant of another, to be made to work at will by another, and to be beaten at will." (Sharma R. S., 2005, pp. 124-125) We can see here, the formation of "in-groups" and "out-groups" at this stage.

The concept of 'dvija' (Leslie, 2003) also clarifies that there were rituals that conferred certain rights and statuses on the three upper castes and not the lower ones. All this point towards the trend, that there was certainly a feeling of 'us and them' with the Brahmans, Kshatriyas Vaishyas on the one side and Kshudras on the other and that these feelings were cemented by rituals and symbols or in other words by a 'culture' that perpetuated such beliefs.

It is however, not true that there were no in-group and out-group currents at work between the three so called 'upper castes' as "sometimes the brahmanas came into conflict with the rajanyas" as per Professor R.S Sharma. However, whenever the two upper orders had to deal with the lower orders, they put aside their differences. Towards the end of the later Vedic period, it began to be emphasised that the two upper orders should cooperate to rule over the rest of the society (Sharma R. S., 2005, p. 124). It could be possible perhaps that gradually, the 'in-group feeling' that was initially limited to the two upper castes also took the third Varna into its fold thereby alienating the fourth varna.

What happened from hereon is the story of a protracted battle between the various castes in India on grounds of ideology, politics, economics and culture.

Stages of Communal separatism[2]

A similar pattern can be traced in the growth of communalism. As opposed to what is generally perceived, the advent of Islam in India was not the herald of communal strife in India. Communal strife seems to have begun with the coming of the heterodox sects of Jainism and Buddhism as offshoots of Hinduism formed by those who considered Hinduism, at it had grown to become during that time, extremely parochial and laden with superstition and rituals. In fact, Ashoka (304-232 BCE) is said to have ordered killings of 18,000 Jains after someone drew a picture of Buddha bowing at the feet of Mahavira. (Jones, 2008). After Independence in the modern era, religious riots have taken place between Hindus, Muslims, Sikhs and Christians with one or more group(s) positioned against the other.

Stage 1: Emergence of a central idea along which a group is formed coupled with the illusion of commonality in all spheres of life (even the spheres are unrelated to the original idea)

Monolithic religions were a novel phenomenon that took place in the human society and eventually provided a strong identifier to the human society that was not based on occupations or territorial considerations but on philosophy or rather culture. At the heart of all religions is a philosophy, which on closer examination is found to have more in common with each other than is usually perceived. However, a way of life or a culture emerges from each of these philosophical traditions that produce different expressions of fundamentally the same values which over-time crystalises into different 'religions'. Philosophers such as Sri Aurobindo and many others as well as historians such as Romila Thapar, R.S. Sharma etc. have famously argued that Hinduism was not a monolithic religion at its inception but was rather a way of life. Similar arguments are resounded in the writings of Talal Asad who argues that Christianity was a disciplina, a "rule" just like that of the Roman Empire. This idea can also be found in the writings of St. Augustine (354–430). Christianity was then a power structure opposing and superseding human institutions... It was the discipline taught by one's family, school, church, and city authorities, rather than something calling one to self-discipline through symbols (Asad, 1993). Once having gained common expressions in terms of symbols, rituals and practices when the religion takes over all phases of life, it reaches the culmination of the first stage of separatism. The religion now becomes more than *just* a philosophy. The 'Tyranny of labels' comes into play here.

Stage 2: Realisation that the group is distinct in all spheres of life and other groups exist that are distinct in every sense and in their interests

Every religion goes through a phase of expansion where it incorporates under its fold new members and spreads in new geographies through its patrons. Those in the new geography accept the new 'way-of-life' offered by the new religion, are taken into its fold and those who choose to stick to their old 'ways-of-life' (notwithstanding the fact that even the old ways will be going through imperceptible changes) are seen as different in all aspects by people of the other religion. The realisation that comes about is not that the philosophies pronounced by the two religions are different but that their symbols, their rituals, their conjugal rights, and in total their cultures are different. The survival instinct of the human being too is ironically programmed as such that differences or newness of a situation and the insecurities that it entails catches attention more than commonalities; or as Daniel Kahneman puts it– "losses loom larger than gains" (Kahneman, 2011) and newness of any situation triggers an insecurity to lose what one has. This encounter between two ways of life, of two cultures triggers the fundamental insecurity ingrained in human nature and the 'other' is preconceived as a threat.

Stage 3: Realisation that the interests and the way of life of other groups are antithetical to those of own group

Once the initial encounter of two religions begins on a note of mutual suspicion, in the absence of a common identity, adequate interaction and common goals and in the presence of at times economic and cultural disparities, a competition between the two ways of life ensues. Lack of resources may not be a necessary precondition for such a competition to take place. After all, the football riots are a perfect example in such a scenario. Fans of two clubs (read religions) engage into banter which leads to brawls between groups of people. What they fight about is not economic resources but on allegiances. The two rival clubs in sports, engage into harmless banters to serious gang brawls while religious clubs fight it out in isolated brawls to mass riots, genocides and wars.

When the realisation of belongingness grows stronger as it happens by the means of religious rituals that serve as constant re-enforcements and reminders of belonging to a particular religious community, the bias for those belonging to own group is also consequently and perhaps proportionately intensified.

Solutions

The issue of resolution of the communal and caste issue in India falls under the broader purview of inter-group conflicts. For the resolution of intergroup conflicts, broadly three measures have been identified. I call this the 3C model of inter-group conflict resolution. The three C's denote – Contact, Common Superordinate Goals and Categorisation.

Contact

The first of these measures is known as the "contact hypothesis" (All port, 1954). In the contact hypothesis, equal status **contact in a neutral environment, enabling members of different groups to form friendships**, is supposed to reduce intergroup tension. In an article "Ethnic Conflict and Civil Society India and Beyond", Ashutosh Varshney contends that "if communities are organised only along intra-ethnic lines and the interconnections with other communities are very weak or even non-existent, then ethnic violence is quite likely" (Varshney, 2001). He further divides civic networks (of contact), both intraethnic and interethnic, into two other types: 'organised and quotidian'. Varshney explains: "This distinction is based on whether civic interaction is formal or not". He calls the formal interactions "associational forms of engagement"—those that include – Business associations, professional organisations, reading clubs, lm clubs, sports clubs, NGOs, trade unions, and cadre-based political parties etc.; and he calls the informal interactions (through quotidian networks) the "everyday forms of engagement" - that consist of "simple, routine interactions of life, such as whether families from different communities visit each other, eat together regularly, jointly participate in festivals, and allow their children to play together in the neighbourhood".

According to Varshney, "both forms of engagement, if robust, promote peace: contrariwise, their absence or weakness opens up space for ethnic violence." Varshney also submits an interesting conclusion, that "Of the two, however, the associational forms turn out to be sturdier than everyday engagement, especially when confronted with attempts by politicians to polarise people along ethnic lines. Vigorous associational life, if interethnic, acts as a serious constraint on politicians, even when ethnic polarisation is in their political interest. The more the associational networks cut across ethnic boundaries, the harder it is for politicians to polarise communities."

Among the earlier proponents of the "contact hypothesis" as a solution to the caste problem in India was Mahatma Gandhi. Mahatma Gandhi, expounded the mantra of 'inter-dining and intermarriage' to ward off the discriminatory mind-set.

However, contact in itself is not enough and may result at times in an increased rather than a reduced sense of mutual animosity and competition. At least as a stand-alone solution, mere contact may not be enough and may sway the dynamics either way–towards cooperation or competition. The mixed results of the school desegregation program in the United States to improve race relations between blacks and whites (Cook, 1985) showed that in real life, mere increased contact between groups is not enough to break down stereotypes and reduce tension.

Dr B.R. Ambedkar wrote an undelivered speech—"The Annihilation of Caste"–prepared as the presidential address for the annual conference of a Hindu reformist group Jat-Pat TodakMandal, on the ill effects of caste in Hindu society[3]. Dr Ambedkar presented his views on the solution to the caste-problem. He only agreed with half of Gandhi's mantra of 'inter-dining and intermarriage'. He found inter-caste dining an "inadequate remedy". Dr Ambedkar added that "There are many castes which allow inter-dining. But it is a common experience that inter-dining has not succeeded in killing the spirit of Caste and the consciousness of Caste." According to him, inter-marriage was the only solution to the problem and that "Fusion of blood can alone create the feeling of being kith and kin, and unless this feeling of kinship, of being kindred, becomes paramount, the separatist feeling—the feeling of being aliens—created by Caste will not vanish". Yet, he found even inter-marriage an impracticable idea. He wrote: "Caste is not a physical object like a wall of bricks or a line of barbed wire which prevents the Hindus from commingling and which has, therefore, to be pulled down. Caste is a notion; it is a state of the mind. The destruction of Caste does not therefore mean the destruction of a physical barrier. It means a notional change." Finally, Ambedkar submitted that: "The real remedy is to destroy the belief in the sanctity of the Shastras."[4,5]

Common Superordinate Goals

The second measure to reduce inter-group conflicts is the presence of common superordinate goals. This approach can also be called the "Superordinate Identity Approach". Sherif, Sherifet. Al. (1961) conducted a landmark research at Robber's Cave:

> They divided a small set of about twenty five normal eleven to twelve year old boys into two groups and allowed freedom to organise their own activities. Within each group a structure emerged, with some boys becoming leaders, and more central to the social network and decision making of the group than others.

Each group developed its own norms for favoured activities and places. After a few days, the two groups of boys were brought into contact with one another under competitive conditions involving mutually incompatible goals. The boys were pitted against one another in sporting competitions for prizes, and were brought into situations like a party where there was food enough only for one group, and one group was invited before the other one. One can imagine the feelings of the boys who arrived expecting a party only to find the other group having eaten all the food. It was found that within-group solidarity was at its peak when intergroup hostility was most severe and that interpersonal associations with members of the other group were no longer tolerated under conditions of intergroup conflict. Now the more conflict oriented boys were preferred as leaders for conflict. One boy previously considered a bully became a hero. Another boy, who was a leader initially, lost his status when he refused to come out to confront the rival group of boys during a raid. In the final phase of the experiment, it was discovered that only a series of superordinate goals was able to reduce the intergroup conflict. The achievement of these goals require the cooperation of both groups. Sherif and his colleagues engineered a series of crises that endangered the ability of the camp to continue, such as threatening the camp's water supply or having supply truck fall into a ditch. They organised the two groups of boys to work together to resolve the crises. For example, boys from the two groups worked together to search for the leak in the water supply, and boys of both the groups were needed to pull the truck out of the ditch. These superordinate goals had the effect of pulling the two groups together, whereas such strategies as sermons by a priest, negotiations between leaders, and joint social activities were ineffective. Throughout the experiment, it was the structure of the situation that dictated behaviour rather than personal preferences. A resolution to conflict was obtained by addressing the conflict situation itself rather than using more interpersonal avenues like improving relationships between the leaders or other group members.

The conclusion that can be derived out of this experiment is that common goals at the local and national level can help dilute the inter-grouprelations in the country. Perhaps conditions where the survival of the community is at stake are those that are conducive to creating of an inter-group cooperation among hitherto competing groups.

However, the question regarding the lasting of this cooperative spirit, once the compelling situational factors are gone or are resolved, seem unanswered. For example, during a war with another nation, or in scenarios as in a competitive sport when India plays off against another nation, the various communities irrespective of religious or caste affiliations come-together to support the nation, however, firstly, this sense of solidarity remains overarching as long as the said situation lasts and relegates into oblivion as the event comes to a close (for example the same people who unanimously fought against the British Raj fought among themselves after the Partition of India); and secondly, such event based opportunities for solidarity are prone to attacks by separatist groups who are on the look-out for outliers and scapegoats. For example, the allegations that a particular group of people did not support the common cause and were in fact sympathetic to the opposition are the stories highlighted by separatists. Any dweller of a small to mid-size town of India would have come across such stories of a particular group living in India not sympathetic to India during a cricket match. What the separatist attempt is to either fabricate false stories or make exceptions look like rules. "All of them, they support the other side, not India...They are all alike" would be a comment that comes from a fundamentalist during the India Pakistan World Cup match in 2015.

Categorisation

Finally, scholars of Social Psychology talk about positive categorisation or re-categorisation as a measure to remove inter-group conflicts which makes up as the third measure for resolution of intergroup conflicts. The underlining logic behind such a suggestion is the dissolving of boundaries between the "in-groups" and "out-groups" by re-categorisation or positive categorisation. This strategy concerns itself with a change of mind-set. One way to do the same is by taking a re-look at the history of the society. Hilton and Liu (2008) have emphasised on the role of history in shaping the world-view of people and in making them identify with and categorise their own selves as, members of one group or another. Hence, it could be argued that interpreting history in a manner that does not criminalise a group and at the same time does not justify the ills of an institution can lead to a more mature understanding of the past and a lesser distance in the psychographic positioning between two groups.

In the case of caste, such an end can be achieved by explaining that 'caste' as an institution was not meant to be evil and to argue that the caste system has outlived its utility (if ever there was one) and hence has to be done away with. Similarly, religion has also been seen as "organised systems of beliefs and practice, with an emphasis on some form of afterlife….(as) a diversion from the real source of oppression in material life" (Habib, 2013). However, over-time it did turn out to be oppressive and excesses were indeed committed.

In fact, here we find two views at play that have been seen as solutions to the problem of intergroup conflicts. The first view is the **"abolition of categorisation"** point of view. Karl Marx indeed envisioned a "class-less, stateless society" which would presuppose the abolition of categorisation of human beings. Gandhi and Ambedkar both, in another context, resounded such a message, though not as extreme as of achieving a classless, stateless society but that of doing away with the caste system (Gandhi) and doing away with caste as well as religion (Ambedkar), though not without much debate. While Ambedkar's position on the subject was more clear and consistent, Gandhi's view kept changing from time to time before reaching a somewhat similar conclusion. Ambedkar said "People are not wrong in observing Caste. In my view, what is wrong is their religion, which has inculcated this notion of Caste"; on the other hand, Gandhi believed that the Hindu Philosophy of 'Varnashrama'[6] did not have a flaw at its inception but that people and changing circumstances had polluted it. Gandhi said: "Caste Has To Go. Varnashrama of the shastras [the Hindu sacred scriptures] is today non-existent in practice. The present caste system is thereby (an) antithesis of varnashrama. The sooner public opinion abolishes it the better." (Lindley)

The second view can be called the **"reformist view"** wherein the basis of division of groups is not sought to be eradicated but to be reformed[7]. This has two further directions, one of forming a new group that is representative of a multitude of groups and second is re-interpreting existing ethos of different groups in a more liberal and tolerant manner. According to J.H. Liu (2012) the primary strategies for reducing intergroup conflict according to identity-based approaches are to attempt to change the basis for self-categorisation to be more inclusive through:

1. interventions attempting to somehow incorporate out-group members into some level of identification with the self, be it as a superordinate category (e.g., "We are all Asians") or
2. as two positively related groups under a superordinate (e.g., blacks and whites thinking of themselves as Americans while at the same time acknowledging themselves as ethnically different) (see Gaertner *et al.,* 1993) - can also be termed as the "Unity in Diversity Approach".

However, it seems that the categorisation approaches can only be successful if they meet the challenge of contradictory claims on the one hand, and through propagation become part of the common belief system of the people at large. A moderate form of re-categorisation has been attempted by those who seek to establish religious sects inviting members from more than one religion. Akbar's experiment in doing so has known to have borne no fruit. Revisionist interpretations of religions that seek to propound a more accommodating and universalistic point of view have on their own fared not too well and remain largely unconvincing. Perhaps there is some truth in what Dr Irfan Habib once said during the K.M. Ashraf Memorial Lecture at Kirori Mal College: "It may seem then, that we have reached a point where it is no longer possible to accommodate modern human values in any religious framework whatsoever; and reason and science must at long last stand on their own." (Habib, 2013).

The role of mass media, art, theatre, education and parentage (even at times propaganda and symbolism) would be critical to the success of this approach. Yet again re-categorisation in the absence of contact and common goals could prove to be futile.

All the three approaches have their own challenges. The first approach is susceptible break-down under extreme pressure as even mixed teams and increased contact may not be able to resist the tension of social strife. The second approach would not be possible without a pressing common goal that forces the conflicting groups to cooperate – a precondition hard to be artificially created or psychologically manufactured and sustained. The last approach though seemingly most sustainable, is perhaps the toughest to execute. Formation or fabrication of superordinate or new positive forms of social categorisation, warding off the challenges to new forms of social categorisation and mass acceptance of such categorisations make the last approach hard to manoeuver.

What is to be done?

In this article an attempt was made to understand the concept of casteism as a subset or as a manifestation of the broader concept of separatism. A framework was then traced to demonstrate how the separatist mind-set grows in a society and takes a self-sustaining form. Finally, a brief attempt was made to delineate the historical growth of casteism in line with the framework of the growth of separatist mind-set that was presented in the article. From the point of view of policy formation, it would be interesting to study how macro-policies can demolish such antagonistic group identities and creating more integrative groups by macro-cultural and symbolic interventions. Finally, we attempted to explore certain theories that seek to explore solutions to inter-group conflict since our diagnosis of the caste problem in India was that it is a problem of separatism which can be categorised as "inter-group conflicts". However, it was concluded that none of the solution as a stand-alone will be sufficient for absolute eradication of inter-group conflicts and only when all three C's – Contact, Common Goals, and re-Categorisation - are present together can a sustainable and tangible solution be sought. However, this is a tough combination to achieve indeed. Some might argue that evoking a spirit of nationalism can be a solution as it would provide people a common identity, many a times common goals and can get people to work together. Yet, nationalism developed to extreme limits has resulted into macro level intergroup conflicts in the form of wars. The only possible solution could perhaps be uniting people to combat tangible issues threatening the humankind in entirety. Issues such as environmental degradation and global warming, poverty, disease etc. so as to foster a culture of 'humanitarianism' can be a possible final solution. Afterall, extreme humanitarianism seems not to have any adverse negative effects. Forming common identities to fight the above mentioned problems would neither be easy nor enough. The eventual solution to the problem would be after all, a realisation on the part of the entire human race of their own nature of forming groups and the outcomes of such a tendency. This solution, from the current point of view seems quixotic enough, but at the same time it is the only way out of the impasse. Perhaps human-beings as a race will mature in their behaviour as the race grows older on the planet.

Afterthoughts

A relevant question that emerges from here is "should human beings be more individualistic and not form groups at all?" The answer to this would perhaps be a "NO" and that perhaps extreme individualism and extreme collectivism would both be detrimental to the society.

Another relevant question that emerges from here is – "should policy formation be tainted by the lenses of separatist ethos?" An obvious answer would be a "NO". However if the question is "should policy formation be cognizant of separatist ethos?" then the answer would be a definitive "Yes". No matter how much we would prefer otherwise, such issues do become influencers in policy formation – positively so, when the policies are directed towards getting rid of these issues altogether by propagating harmony and integration and at other times negatively when policies are formed through the lenses of separatism.

References

1. Strong identification with a group, in fact, influences economic trends as well as outcomes as Akerlof and Kranton(2000)(2005) (2010) have shown, ranging from heterogeneity in preferences (Chen & Li, 2009), differences in prices (Ball, Eckel, Grossman, & Zame, 2001)or conforming to detrimental stereotypes (Hoff & Pandey, 2006). This proves the point that it is in fact, the group mindset that affects economic outcomes. However, the debate whether material milieu shapes the culture or culture shapes the material milieu or whether culture impacts economics or economics shapes culture, is an eternal one (Guiso, Sapienza, & Zingales, 2014). However, the author of the present article is of the inclination that culture and economics is a kind of a chicken and egg story, i.e. culture impacts economics impacts culture.
2. The trajectory of Hindu-Muslim communal conflicts in modern India has been best captured by the historian Bipan Chandra in his book India's Struggle for Independence and shall not be recounted here for the purpose of brevity.
3. However, the speech could not be delivered because Dr Ambedkar's standpoint on caste in the speech "was found by the Reception Committee to be unacceptable" In the afore-mentioned speech, that Ambedkar later got published at his own expense
4. While the word 'Shastra' literally means 'science' or 'methodology', used in a particular context, it came to regarded as a code of conduct for the Hindu society as a whole.
5. We have already discussed the point of view in the previous chapter that the Hindu religion has not any specific design that perpetuates casteism.
6. Refer: Monier-Williams, Monier (2005) [1899]. A Sanskrit-English Dictionary: Etymologically and Philologically Arranged with Special Reference to Cognate Indo-European Languages (Reprinted ed.). Motilal Banarsidass. p. 924.ISBN 9788120831056.
7. Gandhi seems to be an abolitionist in relation to caste but a reformist in relation to religion.

CHAPTER 4

In Search for Equality

The following essay is essentially a compilation of two, based on the theme of socio-economic inequalities in the society. While the first part deals with the question – Is social equality possible? - and takes economic and sociological perspectives and observations into account, the second part deals with a broad theory that charts a pattern of increasing and decreasing inequalities in a society that occur alternatingly. The first part concludes that the market forces more than anything else determine the economic status of an occupation, and of the society at large and that economic inequalities can be reduced but not perhaps done away with because we live in a society wherein complete dependence or complete independence from each other as individuals or as groups is not possible. On the back of these observations, the second part argues that at best, a society can be achieved where the power distance between the highest and the lowest strata may be considerably small and wherein there shall be much socio-economic mobility, but and at the same time volatility of social position for the people. Yet the second part seeks to establish that decreasing and increasing social inequalities are in fact, trends that take form of 'Kondratiev waves' (Barnett, 1998) over a very long period of time. To put it simply, in a highly stratified and unequal society, the level of inequalities decreases, reaches a certain low point and thereafter increase still it reaches a zenith, beyond which it again starts decreasing. This cyclical trend continues in perpetuation and the changes take place over a long period of time in a manner that they are almost imperceptible.

Part 1: Equality[1] and its possibility

The question of social equality has been the central theme of a protracted debate in academia[2]. There are a set of optimistic scholars and thinkers who argue that through the provision of equal opportunities to people (Arneson, 1989) (Roemer, 1998), through state intervention or state control (Thomson, 1949) (Benn, 1959), through mass sensitisation and education (Fishkin, 1983) (Brighouse & Swift, 2009) (Chernyshevsky, 1989), and through political action (Lenin, 1987) equality can indeed be achieved in the society. On the other hand, there are others (Mosca) (Pareto) who take the pessimistic view and who hold that equality is a utopia that can never be achieved.

Pareto had famously declared that "history is a graveyard of aristocracies". Explaining Pareto, Benoît Mandelbrot wrote:

> One of Pareto's equations achieved special prominence, and controversy. He was fascinated by problems of power and wealth. How do people get it? How is it distributed around society? How do those who have it use it? The gulf between rich and poor has always been part of the human condition, but Pareto resolved to measure it. He gathered reams of data on wealth and income different centuries, such as the tax records (of Basel, Switzerland, from 1454 and Augsburg, Germany, in 1471, 1498 and 1512), contemporary rental income (from Paris) personal income from (Britain, Prussia, Saxony, Ireland, Italy, Peru). What he found – or thought he found – was striking. When he plotted the data on graph paper, with income on one axis, and number of people with that income on the other, he saw the same picture nearly everywhere in every era. Society was not a "social pyramid" with the proportion of rich to poor sloping gently from one class to the next. Instead it was more of a "social arrow" – very fat near the bottom where the mass of men live, and very thin at the top where sit the wealthy elite. Nor was this effect by chance; the data did not remotely fit a bell curve, as one would expect if

wealth were distributed randomly. "It is a social law", he wrote: something "in the nature of man". (Mandelbrot & Hudson, 2004)

The two opposite viewpoints – one of Pareto and the other of the egalitarians such as Marx, Engels, Kant etc. seem irreconcilable. However, in my personal view, equality indeed can be achieved in societies and the determinant of equality is inter-dependence that follows a demand—supply paradigm. To understand the same, we shall first study how the imbalance between demand and supply of labour force creates an overall economic and occupational inequality in the society.

Let us try to understand how inequalities are created for different occupational classes. For example, in a manufacturing industry, the labourers are susceptible to low wages and exploitation when their skill set is not scarce (i.e., if one labourer disagrees to work at a certain offered wage rate, a replacement can be found by employing another labourer with negligible switching costs) and secondly when their skill set is easily replaceable through machines without incurring massive switching costs. At the same time, as can be noticed in different trades, the workers who command a much higher wage rate than others are ones whose skills are scarce and not easily replaceable through mechanisation (either due to technological or financial constraints). Here, I take examples from the town of Firozabad in (U.P.), the place I was born and brought up in. Firozabad is known as "India's Glass City" as it is the primary glass manufacturing hub of the country. In a typical glass industry in Firozabad, while a common labourer gets 'x rs.' as a daily wage, the person called a 'blower' who blows into the molten glass through a pipe to give it a shape gets paid far more pay than a regular labourer. The 'blower' is paid a higher wage owing to the scarcity and lack of replaceability of their skill.

However, many would argue that the risk factor involved in performing a job also determines the level of pay for a worker; I believe that a better contention would be to say that the risk factor involved in performing a job should determine the level of pay for a worker but not necessarily does (especially in under-developed industries such as that of Firozabad where government regulations are flouted by many factories). A point to be noted here is that the glass 'blower' is not paid a higher wage because he performs a job that entails occupational hazards, it is because of the low replaceability and scarcity of the skill. The mine-workers working in dangerous and hazardous conditions are not paid a higher wage despite the imminent risk attached to their jobs. While the government regulations do regulate wage rates to try and make up for the differences, there cannot be a government regulation that can decisively say that a worker working in a vehicle manufacturing factory has to be paid lesser than a worker working in the mine, below the ground –i.e. The government fixes lower limits of remuneration in our economy and in comparison, despite the fact that a mine worker has a governmental safeguard regarding a minimum wage, he may still be relatively underpaid because of the market dynamics that fail him. The question here then is – Who decides? And the answer is – a combination of market forces, government action, workers' initiative in different sectors, corporate policy and public opinion. However, market forces are the prime determinant of the position while the other factors act as adjustment levers to change the effect brought about by the market forces and fit the outcome into a society's ideas of justice.

Another argument that seems perceptibly valid but turns out to be only partially true on deeper inquiry is the factor of criticality of a job as a determinant of the levels of remuneration. The criticality of a job in many cases could be subject to perceptions. For example, it is certainly hard to define that whether in a manufacturing organisation, a managerial post has a greater criticality to the overall existence of the organisation or the position of the shop floor workers who engage in the direct production of the material. Nevertheless, while the criticality of the job may differ across times and may be subject to changing perceptions, the perception of criticality does play a role in determining the pay levels for a job.[3,4] Somehow, it plays out in such a manner that the criticality of the management is perceived to be higher than the shop floor workers. However, is it really so? Can such an organisation work without shop floor workers? The criticality of a job is certainly not the factor that determines the pay, but it is the degree of replaceability. The shop-floor workers can be easily replaced by a new set of workers and the management is not as easily replaceable. So a justification that management performs a more critical task and thereby is paid more is an erroneous one. First of all shop floor workers can be easily replaced by a new set of workers at a comparatively low cost, but to replace managers is expensive. Secondly, in future the manual job done by shop floor workers may be replaced by machines or robots but the job of the managers that includes decision making, planning, strategizing etc. will always require human beings.

So when the criticality of a job and the hazards related to a job are either a matter of perception or of ignorance, the market forces at work in the labour market clearly come out as the prime shapers of the remunerations attached to a class of jobs. This is however not tantamount to saying that the demand for a job is essentially guided by rational considerations, but the point here is that the supply of resources (both in terms of replaceability and availability) along with their market demand play a more significant part in determining job-class remunerations than any other factor.

In fact, we may submit that essentially there are three factors that determine the socio-economic position of an occupation:

1. Degree of replaceability – the degree to which the incumbents in an occupation can be replaced by machines, non-human-processes and automations and the levels of switching costs associated with the same.
2. Degree of scarcity – the degree of switching costs from one incumbent to the other and the levels of switching costs associated with the same.
3. The degree of perceived criticality – the degree of actual or perceived threat in case of the absence of the job and/or job incumbent.

In the above-stated model, while the first two points form the supply side of the graph, the last point forms the demand side. It is the interplay of these three factors that determine the price that a society is willing to pay, to the incumbents of a job. As far as an equal society is concerned, it can be formed in a situation when there is equal demand and equal supply for all the occupations in the society. However, such a situation can only be achieved in two types of social settings – to which for ease of understanding, the nomenclature Society I and Society II are assigned in the following paragraphs.

Let us look into these two hypothetical societies one by one to understand the possibilities of the presence of an egalitarian society.

Society I:

Society I has three people completely dependent on each other and with exclusive knowledge of highly critical jobs necessary of all the three's survival.

One is a person who only knows how to catch fish, another is a person who only knows how to light up a fire and a third is a person who only knows how to cook. The only thing available to eat is fish and that too of a variety that has to be cooked to be eaten and is otherwise poisonous.

Let us assume here that the only primary requirement for survival is food in this society, and of course that uncooked food cannot be eaten. Also let us rule out the element of greed for the sake of understanding, and assume that all three of them need and desire equal portions of food in order to survive.

In such a society then, complete equality can be possible since there is no replaceability, where there is scarcity of skill and high criticality of each person's job thereby making it a society of complete interdependence. In such a society, one cannot exploit the other.

Society II:

Society II has three people completely independent of each other. All of them know how to catch fish, make a fire and cook fish. Further, the availability of fish in the sea is abundant and easy which makes society II sound like heaven. In such a society, there would remain no cause for exploitation since there would be a plenty for everyone.

Yet it would not be tough to conclude that the presence of either of these societies in the real world is not possible, hence, the impossibility of an equal society in absolute terms; because the presence of Society I and Society II assumes the following:

- Complete dependence or independence from each other of all individuals
- Equal demand and supply of each job

In a real world the possibility of the presence of the abovementioned factors is almost impossible. Added to the above list is the assumption of the absence of the group formation tendencies so innate to human beings. Studies in psychology show that human beings tend to form groups even many a times on arbitrary basis and have the tendency to discriminate against members of other groups (see Tajfel *et al.*, 1971 and Chen and Li, 2009). Also, it has been proved that mere identification with a group, in fact, influences economic trends as well as outcomes as Akerlof and Kranton (2000) (2005) (2010) have shown, ranging from heterogeneity in preferences (Chen & Li, 2009), differences in prices (Ball, Eckel, Grossman, & Zame, 2001) or conforming to detrimental stereotypes (Hoff & Pandey, 2006). Hence, added to the demographic and economic factors are the factors related to human psychology that serve as impediments to the creation of an equal society.

Yet, like many other theoretical constructs, like the perfect competition market (Mas-Colell, Whinston, & Green, 1995) or the class-less-stateless society (Marx), the egalitarian society serves as an ideal for the people to strive towards. The collective will of the people over centuries have led human beings to form a more egalitarian society, if only in matter of degree, than before. The move from monarchy to democracy, from monopoly to open and competitive markets, are all indicators of the advent of an era of greater liberty enjoyed by more and more people in the world. How much of it has been a direct result of human endeavour is however, debatable, yet the human contribution in bringing about such trends cannot be undermined.

Part 2: The Progression of Equality

The study of world histories throws light upon macro trends of historical progression. A cursory evaluation of world history shows a clear trend that the degree of inequality in societies has followed the path of 'Kondratiev waves' (Barnett, 1998) These waves have been invisible throughout the course of history in the forms of alternating governmental set ups, fluctuating between the rule of one, to the rule of some, and eventually to the rule of many. While the Mesopotamian and Egyptian "Divine Kings" represent the rule of one, the graeco-roman republics represent the presence of the rule of many. The republics then gave rise to local monarchies, which in their turn gave way to a feudal polity of lords and vassals (Farooqui, 2001). At the closing of the feudal period, there was a reassertion of absolutism, followed by enlightened despotism, which was in turn followed by democratic revolutions around the world. This was followed by the advent of colonial regimes that were eventually washed away by a second wave of democratic revolutions. While this may look like an over-simplification of historical trends (it must be admitted that exceptions to these trends have throughout been present), yet a broad description of history in the above mentioned terms would not be grossly mistaken.

A king used to be a person who had all the rights in the world. He had the complete freedom to go anywhere in his domains, had the complete liberty over his time, he was the sole owner of all his dominions, the rest were his tenants, and so he was the only person who had the right to property, his word was the law, he was allowed everything since he was the embodiment of God on Earth. With the advent of feudalism the king had to share his power with a few sub-contractors, now they owned their own lands (in the name of the king) - their fiefs. They came into an agreement with the King that in lieu of the land – the fief – that they have got from the King, they will supply him with a regular stream of revenue in form of taxes collected from their lands and shall also supply the king with arms and men whenever the King calls upon them for service. Consequently, this fragmentation of political power allowed the feudal lord to exercise many rights that were the hitherto exclusive to the monarch. In their own territories, these fief holders or vassals would act as the supreme lords. (They could go anywhere in the territory, their word was the law, they even guided the religion of the people).

With the advent of democracy, the power that was vested in the single person of the King alone began to get distributed among more and more people. At the same time more and more began to gain access to a lot of liberties, such as the right to formulate laws, to own property, to religion, freedom of expression, in the formation of the government. Today, we are in the era of universal suffrage and we have access to a considerable amount of liberties, the fundamental rights allow us to gather anywhere, speak almost anything, reside anywhere in the country, practice any religion. We enjoy to greater or lesser degrees rights that were once only reserved for the person of the King. So basically, all of us are kings, but only of minor forms.

That one man's powers are shared by a vast chunk of population today. Obviously no one has access to the excesses that the original king was allowed, but in our little kingdoms, we do have some rights, obviously some have more rights than the others and some are more equal than the others, but nevertheless, there is more equality now than ever before, at least in comparative terms.

In the earlier times, it was only the kings who followed religion of their choice and led a lifestyle as they wished to lead. Although this is not to say that they were not bound by protocols and code of conducts, but these bindings were not absolute and there are many instances in history where the kings have transgressed these code of conducts which a common man would have not even imagined to do. However, with the disintegration of power from a monarchical rule to feudalistic oligarchies and then to republics and democracies, we notice two trends:

1. The bindings of the code of conducts gradually increase over the kings (those at the helm of the state affairs), then over the nobility and so on
2. Access to liberty for the common man increases over time till a point where an equilibrium of liberty and code of conduct is achieved between the King and the commoner

For example, heads of most of the states today do not have the right of life and property over any other person (in most cases) anymore, as was the rule previously.

It can be concluded that the history of states seems to oscillate between the 'rule of one' to the 'rule of many'. However, one wave of oscillation can be delineated into four successive stages characterised by two trends that come into play and these I have named as:

1. A reduction of power distance[5]
2. A fracturing of the power wall[6]

For the purpose of understanding, I have taken the four social strata/positions–the King, the nobility[7], the bourgeoisie[8] and the commoners[9] as the four levels of social existence in terms of the possession and share of social power per person. While the King is one person who is at the apex of the state and in an individual capacity enjoys greater power than any other person in the society. The nobility while collectively as a class may enjoy even greater power than the King and may have the power to displace the King, yet individually a noble will only hold a lesser degree of power than the King. Similarly, at the individual level, a bourgeois individually shall hold a lesser degree of power than the King and the nobles but a greater degree of power than a commoner. Hence, the removal of the power base of a social position can only take place if one or more strata below it unite to overthrow it. To put it simply, a king can be removed if either as a collective class the nobility, the bourgeoisie or the commoners or a combination of any of them colludes to remove the king. Similarly, any power base can be removed when faced by a united action of a power base or bases that total up to form a greater power. However, these power bases do not remain as distinct and rigid over time as the pendulum of power swings. The pyramid gradually turns into a plateau as time passes by.

Let us understand the concept with the help of the following sequential figures:

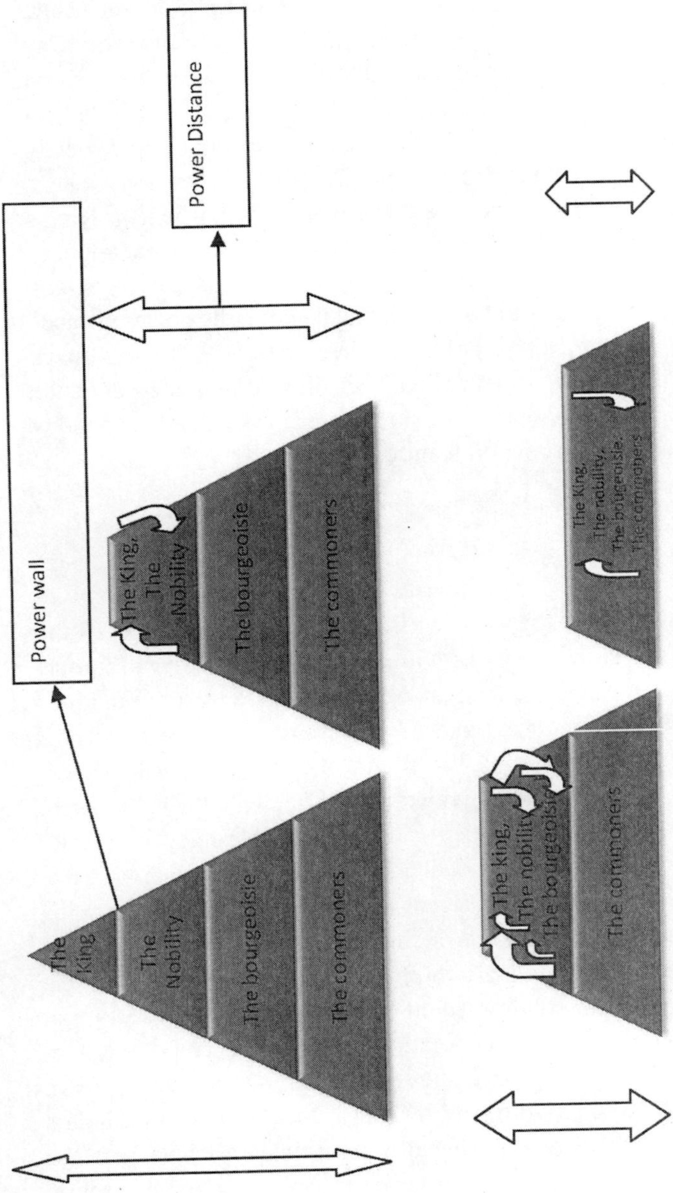
Power wall
Power Distance
The King
The Nobility
The bourgeoisie
The commoners
The King,
The Nobility
The bourgeoisie
The commoners
The king,
The nobility
The bourgeoisie
The commoners
The King,
The nobility,
The bourgeoisie:
The commoners

Stage One

In the above figures, in stage one the power walls are intact and rigid allowing minimal transgression and social mobility. The King is at the apex of the pyramid, has a distinct identity and his position is entrenched by sheer force and/or by birthright and sanctified by a divine right philosophy. There are widespread examples of a society in the first stage such as the Mauryan Emperors, The early Guptas, the early Tsars of Russia etc. These were the states in which the King's word was the law and the King's power came mostly by birthright or victory in war rather than by the acclaim of the nobility or strata. Since at this stage, as can be seen in the diagram, the power distance between the king and the nobility is less, therefore, it would have been hardly avoidable to maintain absolute dominance over the nobility and certainly a power tussle between the king and the nobility would have been a common feature.

Stage Two

In stage two the pyramid becomes flatter and the King now shares power with and exercises authority with the help of a larger base of aristocracy as was the case with feudalism. Hence, due to the weakened and cash-strapped environment of early medieval Europe, "standing armies or permanent officer corps were unthinkable" (Strayer 1970, 27) for a centralised authority to maintain. Thus, feudalism, characterised by its "fragmentation of political power" (1970, 14), emerged whereby rulers would rule with the help of sub-agents.[10] That was the time when an individual noble enjoyed a greater share of power than an individual noble would have earlier. Also this stage is characterised by different sections of nobility influencing the appointment of the king or the head of the state. Therefore, instances of Kings bringing into prominence new groups of people into the fold of the nobility would have been a common feature in these societies, so that one section of the nobility proves as a counterweight to the other. Studies conducted by I. A. Khan (1968), M. Athar Ali (2001), Firdos Anwar (Anwar, 2001) and other scholars on the composition of the Mughal nobility clearly show how the Mughal emperors would counterweight the influence of one section of the nobility by another. Similar examples could be found in the court of the Tsars. The point to be remembered here is that for the king to maintain his rule, it is imperative that he keeps the nobility divided for the nobility together forms a greater power chunk than the king. If however, during this stage the nobility got together, they could remove the king if the king was unable to garner support from another power base that can be united to counterbalance the power of the nobility. It is therefore, perhaps why Machiavelli had advised his Prince never to be hated or despised by the public[11] (The Prince). In the threat of being overthrown by the nobility, the only hope for the king to remain at the throne would be to combine strata(s) of bourgeoisie and/or the commoners to displace the nobility.

Stage Three

In stage three, the pyramid becomes even flatter and now, a section of businessmen of bourgeois backgrounds seek ennoblement and have an active say in matters of the government and thereby become active contestants of power. In this stage many erstwhile nobles get reduced to a bourgeois status and many former bourgeois rise up (or try to rise up) to the status of nobility (McPhee, 2002). As pointed out by scholars the ennoblement of the bourgeoisie was widespread in seventeenth century France. In fact the power base of the bourgeoisie became so strong by the eighteenth century in France that a ban was placed on any further ennoblements by office after 1728 (Heller, 2006). This would have been a response to keep the bourgeois power from consolidating and an attempt must have been made to muster support from other power bases to keep the bourgeoisie from capturing more power–and indeed such was the case as a wave of re-feudalisation had hit France at the close of the seventeenth century in an attempt to take power from the new nobility by the traditional one.

Indeed, such attempts to contain the bourgeois bid for power could not sustain for long. Just as the king and the nobility became more and more of a common pool in Stage I, in Stage II the King, the nobility and the bourgeoisie would be mashed in together to fall in the same pool.

By the close of the eighteenth century, mercantilism was at its peak -- a key feature of the European states of the time (Sinha, 2010). As Irfan Habib (1972), Om Prakash (1987) and Najaf Haider (2002) have pointed out, the monetisation of the Indian economy that received a boost from sixteenth century onwards (just like the European mercantilism that developed from the onset of the sixteenth century) had matured to a considerable level by the eighteenth century. By the nineteenth century with the ushering of the industrial revolution, the bourgeoisie had broken the power walls of the society to a considerable extent and gradually the nobility was now to be seen to emulate bourgeois lifestyles and entering bourgeois professions. In fact "Over the course of the eighteenth century the model of the courtier would be substituted by a new conduct code that was diverted towards the promotion of the new middle classes" (Cruz, 2006). The plateau of social power was getting ever flatter as from now on, the king, the nobility and the bourgeoisie would comprise a social class meddled into each other. The power distance between the head of the state and the bourgeois was not as much as it used to be and in fact the bourgeoisie now started playing an active role in defining the power dynamics of the society. The bourgeoisie had now become a "Klassefuersich (class in itself)"[12]. Currently, we seem to be in this stage wherein while there is a rich poor divide, yet the power distances are constantly getting contracted. At the helm of the state affairs, the bourgeoisie is finding membership and those who are beginning to or are already influencing the state are the commercial classes. The once looked down upon merchant can now live more lavishly than the head of a state. And indeed heads of states are gradually emerging from the bourgeois ranks. In this stage, when the Kings fall they open businesses and when businesses rise, they strive to rule the state[13].

Stage Four

The stage four entails the breaking of all the power walls and creates a situation of high social mobility. This stage can be characterised by:

1. Extremely high degree of social mobility
2. Greater number of rags to riches cases

3. Greater number of riches to rags cases
4. A state of social flux wherein hierarchical relations become radically redefined

I suspect that we still have not reached a stage such as that of the stage 4 but are certainly heading towards it. We are living in an age when people from the bourgeoisie are playing ever greater roles in defining the power structures. At the same time the commoners are also entering mainstream politics and are gradually asserting their will in forms of direct democracies. Hence, we currently seem to be somewhere between stage 3 and stage 4.

Once the stage 4 reaches a maturation point, it can be hypothesised that it will then give way to a new form of the third stage, which in turn will pass into a new form of second stage and eventually the first one. The pendulum of history and thereby social equality shall again move in the direction of inequality and in the long run shall again turn towards equality.

However, it is hard to say that even in stage 4 there will absolutely no power distances. It is just that there will be greater possibility for everyone to reach the uppermost power layer.

Yet, we may well agree that we have come a long way from the times when all the power of the state was invested in the person of the king, to a new world where the same amount of power which was once enjoyed by a single person, has been divided – unequally though, among many. More and more nations these days believe in the fundamental human rights of a person irrespective of his socio-economic background. The Right to Life, the Right to Freedom, the Right to Equality with which people are born with today, were not even present in theory in earlier centuries. 'Rights' even in theory were the monopoly of only a few who formed the uppermost layer of the society.

Thus while, it is argued, that capitalism has increased the power distance among the rich and the poor we may well argue that the overall distance between the rich and the poor has reduced in a capitalistic society. The "power walls" are being fractured. In the nineteenth century, as remarked by Reverend R. Parkinson on the condition of the employed at Manchester, that: "There is far less personal communication between the master cotton spinner and his workmen, between the calico printer and his blue handed boys, between the master tailor and his apprentices, than there is between the Duke of Wellington and the humblest labourer on his estate, or than there was between good old George the Third and the meanest errand-boy about his palace" (1841). Such was the case in the mid-nineteenth century. Only a century later, however, we could see examples of workmen becoming master craftsmen, blue handed boys becoming calico printers, apprentices becoming tailors,–all owners of big firms-not to forget the gas station attendant rising up to become one of the richest men in the world. The trend of dissipation of power walls, though more visible currently in the developed economies, is swiftly spreading in the developing nations and may soon engulf the entire world.

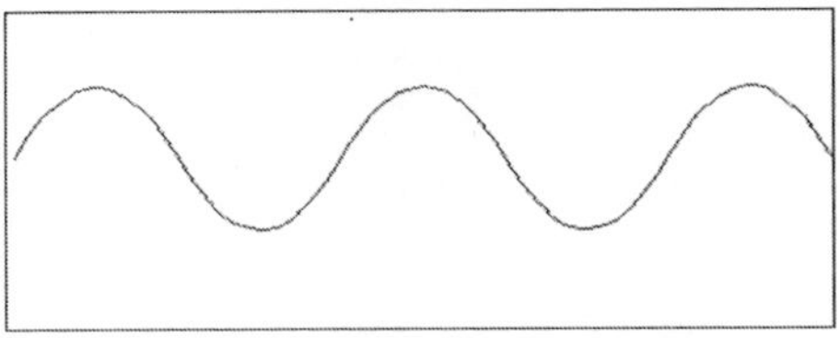

Conclusion

The argument here is that the power distance is getting reduced and the access to liberties viz. the bindings of code of conducts are getting equalised. Therefore, we may say that we are moving towards a society where in the privileges of the monarch are being replicated a multiple times and to various degrees among the common population. On the one hand, the concentration of liberty decreases from the topmost rung, it percolates down to the lower orders hence bringing them upwards. Thus, we are moving towards "commonisation". Nevertheless, the limitations of human interventions in determining the course of history should be if not accepted, then, at least apprehended and as human beings, the moral responsibility of curbing injustices and atrocities over the disadvantaged must be avoided. A sense of realisation above all has to come, that as a race human beings cannot wait for an equal society to arrive – the historical waves shall widen and shorten the cleavage of inequality. As evolved and thinking creatures, it is the responsibility of the human being to ride on the waves of history, bound by a spirit of mutual respect that is unperturbed and not dependent on material dependence or independence on and from each other. It is the responsibility of human beings to get stronger in its organisational capacity and values to prevent injustices against disadvantaged sections when historical waves attempt to usher civilisation into inequalities. At the same time the responsibility in times of low inequalities is to understand ways to sustain social mobility and equality and to prepare to replicate the learnings in times when historical forces attempt to force inequalities over human beings.

References

1. The term 'Equality' has been used throughout the article in the sense of economic and political egalitarianism.
2. (Albernethy, 1959) (Bedau, 1967) (Brown, 1988) (Callinicos, 2000) (Hajdin, 2001) and many more researchers and philosophers have debated about this subject.
3. Yet, various job evaluation methods (HayGroup, 2005) claim legitimacy by using a combination of factors such as accountability, skills, working conditions etc. but still fail to remove the subjectivity in evaluating the attributes and criticality of the jobs.
4. To understand different methods of Job Analysis and Job Evaluation see (Milkovich & Newman, 2005).
5. Power distance refers to the way in which power is distributed and the extent to which the less powerful accept that power is distributed unequally. See (Hofstede, 2001).
6. I define power wall as the socio-economic barriers that restrict mobility from one socio-economic strata to another.
7. In the sense of **'aristocracy' = The highest class in certain societies, typically comprising people of noble birth holding hereditary titles and offices** (http://www.oxforddictionaries.com/definition/english/aristocracy).
8. The middle class, typically with reference to its **perceived materialistic values or conventional attitudes**(http://www.oxforddictionaries. com/ definition/english/bourgeoisie).
9. In the sense of **the 'proletariat' = Working-class people regarded collectively** (http://www.oxforddictionaries. com/definition/english/ proletariat).

10. http://web.stanford.edu/~blaydes/feudal.pdf
11. Also see (Skinner, 2013).
12. Original thought by Karl Marx. For reference, See: (Borland, 2008).
13. Atleast the trends point in these directions, though it may not be a general rule.

CHAPTER 5

The Changing Courses of History

The quest for power has often been a source of conflict in any society. Power led to the world war, power it was that divided the great nation of India. It was nothing but power that motivated Napoleon, Alexander and the likes to conquer far-away lands. Power however, is not to be seen in a negative light here—It is a social reality, it is a human need. It is a social reality in the sense that power is the ability to get things done – now if one wants to get things done for a purpose that is considered noble he becomes a Gandhi, Nehru or a Mandela (they needed power to overthrow an oppressive rule) and if one uses power for a negative motive one becomes a Hitler, Napoleon or a Mussolini. Power is a human need too as research has suggested. According to researchers such as David Mclelland human beings have three needs namely – need for affiliation, need for achievement and *need for power*. Power, it has been accepted is one of the basic human needs. Hence accepting power as a reality is a first step in understanding its dynamics.

Every society strives towards an equitable distribution of power, certain possible historical patterns and trends about which have been discussed in the previous essay. In this essay an attempt will be made to discern the nature of power in different eras of social and historical evolution.

The Four Forms of Power

Power means different things to different people and in different situations. There is a time when the need of the hour is **Expert Power**, at another times **Coercive Power**, at times **Reward Power** and still at other times **Referent Power**[1]. In other words, the four bases of power could be **knowledge, coercion, reward** and **values/personal attributes**. Different people may have preference for different types of power. Similarly, different situations or stages of historical development call for different types of powers.

In different stages of historical development a particular form of power out of the four–knowledge, coercion, reward and values/ personal attributes—is more required than the other. That is however not to say that the other three forms of power are not required in the given situation, it is only that a particular period is marked by a particular form of power. For example, let us say during a war all four forms of power are required – knowledge and expertise is needed to manage resources, gather intelligence and create technology; coercion over the enemy is needed to win in the battlefield; rewards are required to keep soldiers motivated and are also required to garner support of other entities (nations) to fight by your side; and finally a moral ground or appreciable attribute(s) is needed to keep oneself and others convinced to carry out the war along with people who are ready to render service to their nation. Some of the readers may have already started doubting the validity of postulate regarding the requirement of a moral ground to fight and/or win the war. My question in such a case would be – could Arjuna have won or even fought the Mahabharata without being convinced himself about the moral correctness or without the perception of moral correctness of his involvement in the battle? Or could Churchill, Roosevelt and Stalin won the world war had they not convinced the world (and citizens of their own nations) about their moral correctness of being in the war. However, the fact is that even Hitler could not have convinced his nation to wage war on the world had they not believed in his moral correctness. Here the question is of belief and not correctness in any objective terms. Nevertheless, coming back to our original point, while war needs all four forms of power, it would not be an exaggeration to say that war is marked by the power of coercion. Hence, majority of the people who are at the helm of the war machinery are masters in the art of coercion or violence or defence or simply–war-than anything else.

The Age of Knowledge

While war is an extraordinary situation, different eras of history are also marked by different forms of power. In early societies where the human being was completely at the mercy of nature the knowledge for survival would be the greatest power a society would desire. The knowledge of how to save oneself from rain, of how to make fire, of what to eat and what not to—all this knowledge would have been extremely important for a society to survive. Indeed, warriors would also be required to protect against animals, competing species and rival tribes, yet it must not be forgotten that the human being was not yet in a position to play a dominating role in the world as it does now and hence the knowledge of ways to escape, which caves to hide in etc. would have been much more important than the ability to fight. Hence, at the beginning of any society it is knowledge that characterises the dominant source of power. Hence, it is no surprise that the early kings in Ancient Mesopotamian civilisation were 'priest kings' and the state as has been described by some historians–a 'temple state'. The presence of Brahmins as a dominant class during the Ancient Indian history also points towards the same trend.

The Age of Coercion

However, as a civilisation matures and structures become more entrenched; and the most lucrative lands and resources become occupied by one kingdom or the other (or one state or the other), competition begins to occupy the land of the others and that certainly puts different groups of people into conflict. Here if a group is fortunate enough to find new uninhabited lands a fight is avoided, else warfare becomes the key characteristic of the society from then on. Yet after the age of the priest kings – an age of the warlord king descends. It is this age that we remember in our general reminiscence of the past and in doing so we perhaps assume that at the head of the state–or the dominant class of the past–was essentially a warrior;

ignoring the possibility that perhaps there was a time when warriors were not as much needed in the society as were people of knowledge. However, with the change of the social needs there would also have been a change of nobility or the dominant class in the society. In the age of warriors, the erstwhile nobles would have tended towards being more warrior-like to maintain their claim to usefulness for the society and the warriors would have, at the beginning of the stage strived to become accepted into the erstwhile nobility through ennoblement and priestly sanction. Of course, when the warriors would eventually gain sanction as a 'divine ruler' and the sanction of the priestly class would have become only a perfunctory formality, the society would have by then matured into a stage where total dominance of the warrior class would characterise the same.

The Age of Commerce

After a long period of warring, when most of the kingdoms and their boundaries are more or less stabilised (which is not to stay that absolute stabilisation of boundaries occur, as there always are changes, but now fewer ones than before) and the entrepreneurship in building a new state becomes more and more difficult a new form of entrepreneurship emerges – the age of capital descends.What if you cannot be a king of a state? You can now have a kingly status through commercial enterprises. It is in this stage where the Japanese Samurais began to lose their relevance in the society and were reduced to the status of an impoverished nobility of the past. As discussed in the previous chapter, it was in this stage that

> ...a section of businessmen of bourgeois backgrounds seek ennoblement and have an active say in matters of the government and thereby become active contestants of power. In this stage many erstwhile nobles get reduced to a bourgeois status and many former bourgeois rise up (or try to rise up) to the status of nobility (McPhee, 2002). As pointed out by scholars the ennoblement of the bourgeoisie was widespread in seventeenth century France. In fact the power base of the bourgeoisie became so strong by the eighteenth century in France that a ban was placed on any further ennoblements by office after 1728 (Heller, 2006). This

would have been a response to keep the bourgeois power from consolidating and an attempt must have been made to muster support from other power bases to keep the bourgeoisie from capturing more power – and indeed such was the case as a wave of re-feudalisation had hit France at the close of the seventeenth century in an attempt to take power from the new nobility by the traditional one. Indeed, such attempts to contain the bourgeois bid for power could not sustain for long and by the close of the eighteenth century, mercantilism was at its peak – a key feature of the European states of the time (Sinha, 2010). As Irfan Habib(1972), Om Prakash(1987) and Najaf Haider(2002) have pointed out, the monetisation of the Indian economy that received a boost from sixteenth century onwards (just like the European mercantilism that developed from the onset of the sixteenth century) had matured to a considerable level by the eighteenth century. By the nineteenth century with the ushering of the industrial revolution, the bourgeoisie had broken the power walls of the society to a considerable extent and gradually the nobility was now to be seen to emulate bourgeois lifestyles and entering bourgeois professions. In fact "Over the course of the eighteenth century the model of the courtier would be substituted by a new conduct code that was diverted toward the promotion of the new middle classes" (Cruz, 2006).

Even when the colonialists came to India they had a mixed sort of a character–somewhere between a merchant and a warrior. Their state also characterised such a mixture throughout.

Yet, the shifting of gears from one stage to the other is so imperceptible that one can hardly point out a period and say this is where a new age began. This can be noticed in the transition from the stage of War to the age of Capital (we only discuss this transition, since this is the stage that is most fresh in our experience of history). The age of capital seems to have begun in Europe when it saw the transition from a natural economy to the rise of a market economy in the late feudal era. Yet the age of war for Europe (and perhaps for most of the world ended in Second World War more or less and even to a greater degree the same more or less ended after the culmination of decolonisation of states. Coming up with new nations as one would agree is more difficult now than it would have been a few centuries back. More people who seek power today get into businesses than politics. Yet another characteristic of power is that one form of power can, foster and facilitate the growth of another.

The Age of Service

Coming back to our topic, we may again notice a change which is already happening in our society wherein a huge amount of the top leadership of the corporate sector is comprised of not the owners of the firms, but those employees who earn money by selling their labour, skills etc. to the huge corporate houses–The CEOs. Nevertheless, the basis of power is still that of the capital, yet the focus of building capital is gradually and sometimes speedily shifting towards the service sector. In any case, businesses are now more than any other times are influencing policy formation (which is not to say whether it is for the better or worse). It is in this age that we are currently living in.

Another change that marks the current age is a growing concern of the corporates towards social welfare as corporate social responsibility has risen up the corporate agenda in recent years. Finally, a time may come (and some may even argue that it has, while I believe it is yet to arrive), wherein most industries would be saturated and dominated by some big fours or big fives and entering a market with a new enterprise would become a challenge and hence a rarity. In any case opening a new commercial enterprise would perhaps become less and less lucrative and more difficult in that particular stage. New forms of organisations would emerge in such a stage that will open new avenues for people to come at par with the big businessmen. Perhaps, it will be the age wherein individual contributors not only comprising of doctors, lawyers and architects, but even electricians, plumbers etc. would be at the helm of the society. Trends in that direction may already be visible. This will be a time when a typical owner of a business firm would be characterised as fundamentally an individual contributor or serviceman as opposed to merely the owner of capital. Sounds like Steve Jobs? The ennoblement of a new form might have already started and soon perhaps the old nobility may lose its position. The blue chips will still remain and the rest will either seek service based employment or shall become impoverished. This phase may be termed as the stage of the 'nobility of the proletariat', not in the manner how Marx would have envisaged it to be, i.e. not through an apocalyptic war against the bourgeoisie, but rather through a gradual and imperceptible change in the course of history and at times even emanating through the bourgeoisie (an English Revolution of a new form). The major source of power in this age would be referent power. While people possessing other forms of power would still be important in the society, the social power structure will be marked by referent power than anything else.

One might at this stage think that during the age of supremacy of referent power, knowledge itself will be the key characteristic of power, yet I would like to differ with such an argument. Indeed knowledge will impact at this stage the degree of referent power one achieves – the influence of knowledge will most certainly be present as it shall be the next stage in line, yet at that stage (the stage of referent power dominance) brand or a reputation of delivering what has been promised, will be a greater defining factor of power than knowledge.

The Cycle of History

Basis the observation of how the meaning of power has changed (as discussed in the previous section), if one might notice a progression in macro-history, then four basic forms or stages characterised by four different forms of power would be visible–

A peculiarity of such a trend is that whenever history has progressed in a stage-wise manner, change has been smooth and even imperceptible. It does not however matter at which point the cycle begins, or at which speed does the wheel turn, what matters is the order of the cyclical progression of history. However, the times when due to human interventions, an attempt has been made to skip stages or tinker with the order of progression depicted above, there has been much bloodshed and an auto correction of historical development seems to have taken place. This is most noticeable in the case of Soviet Russia.

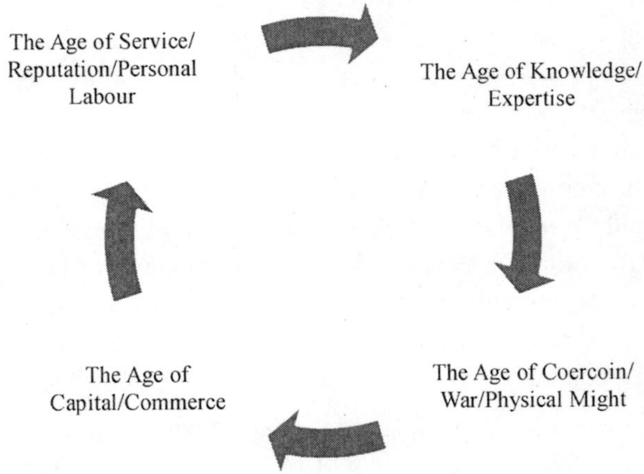

Cyclical progression of history

The problem with Soviet Russia was that it transgressed the order of change. It attempted to bring in socialism before running completely through all the stages of capitalism. It might have been prudent to speed up the development of capitalism to quickly mature to socialism, much like what China is doing today. But by skipping a few stages of capitalism and jumping into socialism they gave birth to a premature and deformed child (And may be the stage that is being discussed here is a socialism which lies outside any of the theoretical constructs of socialism hitherto provided). The result was that the power distances[2] among the various social stratas which would have perhaps reduced over time did not get reduced and only the power wall (the wall that defines the restriction on social mobility from one strata to the other[3]) was assumed to be broken when it had not. In simple words, a situation was created in Russia wherein the social dynamics were expected to change without any actual breakage of the class barriers. Hence, it was an experiment that was ahead of its times and hence premature.

History Repeats Itself?

Perhaps after the 'age of service' as we have called it along with other names that combined together define the age we are entering in, the 'age of knowledge' will re-emerge since there will be so many providers of services; and services that they provide would be so critical that their knowledge and people's trust in their knowledge would be the differentiating factor. This will eventually give way to expertise and knowledge being the key characteristic of social power.

However, another characteristic of these four bases of power is also noteworthy – all these four forms of power have different degrees of volatility. A person can lose his ability to provide service (as well as the reputation attached to the individual's ability) in the society very easily, losing capital would be more difficult, losing physical might or coercive power even tougher and losing knowledge the toughest. At the same time gaining knowledge is perhaps the toughest, gaining coercive power tough but not as much as gaining knowledge, gaining capital comparatively easier and gaining a good perception in front of others (even for a small while) the easiest.

Other Applications of the Fourfold Theory

Career

Yet the presence of these four forms of power represent four ways through which one can progress in a career for the benefit of oneself and others (others too, if power is directed at the right cause). After gaining knowledge one may gain through it other powers and abilities such as-influence and respect, control over means, success in trade and finally exclusive service to the society. Or one might chose to gain wealth first, from wealth a good self-brand, using their good name get people to share their expertise and through expertise power to influence outcomes. Similarly, one can graduate from one mode of power to build another, based on circumstance and preference.

Understanding the Varna System (Perhaps more in philosophy, less in practice)

In fact, this fourfold pattern leads one to suspect that perhaps the Varna system in Indian society was not a representative of a social hierarchy, but was that of the four forms of duties one can do for the society. There was, as has been discussed in the first chapter—no hierarchy; as the philosophy of Varna could have in reality been represented in form of a circle in cyclical movement rather than a pyramid or a ladder.

Theoretical Challenges

Semblance of other similar theories. At this point one may think of drawing similarities between the theory presented here and that formulated by Prabhat Ranjan Sarkar and Ravi Batra who argued that the forms of power manifests itself in social classes representative of four categories of people namely – the Warriors, the Acquirors, the Intellectuals and the Labourers. However, the theory presented in this paper differs from that of Sarkar and Batrais, as firstly, it does not follow the same order as that suggested by Sarkar–it follows the order of knowledge, martial might, possession of resources and possession of a good name and the ability to provide service (brand/respect). Secondly, the theory presented here does not attempt to sketch and establish specific periodisation of eras marked by power forms. Since for different societies, the situation could be a different one. For example, the age of capital matured in some parts of the world earlier than others. Also, it does not seek to classify people into water-tight compartments.

Shall we talk numbers?

The problem of periodicity is specifically tempting and at one point of time I did sit down to put labels to broad periods of history based on the eminent form of power in that era. In fact, I did initially come up with a conclusion that each era roughly lasts some 2500 years with one major fracture in the middle of that era which heralds the parallel rise of the power next in order. However, the attempt was futile since not much data could be found to support any form of periodisation, especially with regards to the shift from the age of knowledge to the age of war. The current shift that we are going through is so close to us that analysing the same is rendered impossible. Hence, I chose to leave this theory at an interpretational level notwithstanding temptations that still affect me as I write. Nevertheless, there is no claim of as to when the next stage will arrive, while there is a sense that we are already on our way to a new era.

The Problems and Side Effects of Power

Power may be compared to an energy drink. It gives the energy to function but it may have side effects nonetheless. A known side effect of power is the creation of 'empathy gap' as per researches conducted in the Kellogg School of Management by Adam Galansky and others. Empathy gap means that the amount of power one has inversely proportional to the degree of readiness to understand others' perspectives or needs. At the same time power also reduces the 'bystander effect' as per the research, i.e. powerful people may be more ready to take action to help a person in distress. This is good news since Daniel Kahneman in his book 'Thinking Fast and Slow' has talked about a research which has shown that not as many people will offer help to a person in distress, as one might think (the pioneering work on the 'bystander effect; has been done by John Darley and Bibb Lalatne in a 1968 research). The research was designed in a manner which goes somewhat like this–a group of people would be divided into two and seated in two separate rooms. One person from each room would get up and would talk over a phone to a person in the other nearby room. Unexpectedly the other person will complain during the course of the conversation, of a pain in the chest and will feign a heart-stroke. Knowing well that the other person is only in a room nearby, not many people from the first room rushed to help the 'person in distress', in the other room. The thinking behind it was the assumption that there are others in the room where the person has suffered the stroke and those people in the other room would help the person in distress. On the other hand, when introductory videos of the people in the first room were shown to independent observers, they over-estimated the number of people who would go out to help the person in distress. Hence, if these conclusions are combined with those of Galansky, one could argue that a person who has a sense of power about oneself may be three times more likely to help another person in distress. In fact, when in a 2008 interview Aubrey Henretty asked Galansky the question – "So when does power make a good leader great?" Galansky's response was "It's when power and perspective taking combine". An argument to enhance perspective taking in international law has been of great concern in recent times. It has been observed that nations that are more dominant in international politics at times fail to appreciate the perspectives and cultural nuances of those that are not as dominant. This leads to certain biases in formulations of international laws. The critical analysis and solutions to such a problem have been discussed in the essay at the end of the book (see Appendix article).

Solutions

In any case, a general consensus seems to prevail around the fact as was discussed at the beginning of the article that power may lead to injustice–especially when the same is distributed unevenly. How is a society to cope with the ill-effects of power? David McClelland seems to have answered that for us. The evil effects of power can be counterbalanced by expanding in the same proportion as that of power, the need for achievement and the need for affiliation in the society. A general prevalence of the need for achievement will keep excesses of power in check as there will be more and more people laying their claims on power from all direction, through all means of power; and a churning of the elite will continuously take place. However, only a greater need for achievement would not be enough because if there is an acute need for achievement and a need for power in the society but no need for affiliation and collaboration the society will be constantly at war with itself. Hence, if power is an energy drink with side effects, certain supplements are required to balance out the side effects, these are –

1. Empathy (that comes from greater exposure and understanding of things that are different to one's own – an

understanding of others' cultures, their problems, their aspirations etc.)

2. A greater need for achievement or rather a need for greater achievement (that goes beyond petty personal gains)
3. A greater need for affiliation and collaboration

The question here arises, how is a society to ensure that all these three needs are present in the right quantities? After all, it is easier to theorise than execute a tangible solution. The role of the government will be critical in this aspect. A government that is ready to ensure that a particular class does not become entrenched as elite even after outliving their utility, a government that is ready to empower people and provide equal opportunities, and a government that can fuel the population with an ambition to achieve something big and a government which is able contain inter-group conflicts and promote harmony and mutual understanding will essentially be the one that will ride on the waves of history most smoothly. Such a government will be able to use its power in a constructive manner.

References

1. See works on this subject by John R.P. French and Bertram Raven (1959); I have excluded the fifth (rather the first) form of power discussed by French and Raven, i.e. 'Legitimate Power' since legitimacy is more of a commonly held idea and while legitimate power does hold value, the current theory focuses more on the powers which emanate through personal competencies.
2. As shown in the sequential pyramidal diagrams in the previous chapter.
3. As shown in the sequential pyramidal diagrams in the previous chapter.

Chapter 6

The Role of Leadership—Cases, Stories and Theories

A society is created not merely on the base of circumstances, neither on the base of merely the will of its leaders, nor merely is it created on the base of ideas. It is the combination of all these three forces working in tandem that lays the foundation of a society and characterises it. Leaders often have an immeasurable role to play in defining the character of a society since they lead not merely people, but even events and circumstances, also ideas. Have leaders who desire to create an egalitarian and unified society–you have a society characterised by unity, amity and equality (let us call it Group +ve); have leaders who desire inequity and separatism (let us call it Group –ve) – internecine antagonisms is all you have. Indeed, history moves through in its own patterns and historical forces shape events, societies and people, but it is the leaders and the people of the society who can in their own turn direct, control and give shape to the forces of history. The leaders make choices as to how they shall use the power they have, they make such choices by understanding the forces of history and through that cognisance they can take the best course possible.

However, the defining character of a society is often a battle between the forces of Group +ve and Group -ve. As in any battle, the outcome is decided by the quality of leadership each side has. When the quality of leadership is better in Group +ve equality and unity prevails and when group –ve has better leaders, bitterness and inequity reign. Outcome in a battle does not favour values, but favours capability. Hence, it would be imperative for a society to have more competent leaders in the Group +veinorder to have a society that is geared for healthy development and peace.

In that case it would be worthwhile to understand how more and more good leaders can be developed to join the cadres of Group +ve.

A discourse to fathom the meaning of Leadership

Research in leadership can be broadly categorised into the following categories –

1. Those that hold that leadership is in born and cannot be learned.
2. Those that hold that leadership is a set of traits that can be learned and developed.
3. Those that hold leadership is situational and different situations demand different types of leaders; even this is divided into further two categories:
   a. Those that hold that different situations demand different types of leaders but leaders who are fit for a particular situation cannot be developed to fit into leadership positions called upon by new situations.
   b. Those that hold that different situations demand different types of leaders and the same leaders can be developed to lead in different kinds of situations.

The first set of theories seem flawed as they fail to explain as to how certain leaders (for example Napoleon) were able to win through their leadership skills throughout their careers and with the same set of skills lost at critical junctures. The second theory seems correct on the surface but when seen in entirety, it entails two assumptions:

1. Certain specific traits are leadership traits and not the others.
2. Having more and more of a particular set of leadership traits enhances a person's leadership capability?

As a talent management consultant, I experienced the fact that is held as a leadership philosophy of many organisations–that one size does not fit all. If a person is for example a good financial manager, it is not necessary that the same person will be good at sales too. Revolutionaries are a classic example in such cases. It can be observed in many histories that the set of people who bring about a revolution and a new state fail to be the best administrators of the state and the state falls apart in jeopardy. The rise of Napoleon owes much to this fact. The revolutionaries of the French Revolution, while they had the competencies to bring about a revolution and strip down the 'Ancient' Regime, did not know how to build a new structure to replace the old one and hence a vacuum was created. This vacuum was filled in by Napoleon, who in turn brought about a counter revolution and France merely returned to its old ways only with a new monarch at the top. What Napoleon offered at this juncture was a structured governmental system which however, did not come out to be much different from the earlier structure. Hence, Alfred Cobban has preferred to call it the "myth of the French Revolution" as nothing that the French Revolution stood for actually took place, France was merely an old wine in a new bottle.

The second theory is also erroneous as it assumes that if risk taking is a leadership trait then a person who takes more and more risk possesses a greater leadership capability. However, a person who is a reckless risk taker can end up causing more harm than good. In this regard the view held by Sun Tzu seems closer to the truth: "That leadership is a matter of **intelligence**, **trustworthiness**, **humaneness**, **courage** and **discipline**. Reliance on intelligence alone results in rebelliousness. Exercise of humaneness alone results in weakness. Fixation on trust alone results in folly. Dependence on the strength of courage results in violence. Excessive discipline and sternness in command leads to cruelty. When one has all five virtues together, each appropriate to its function, then one can be a leader".

However, even Sun Tzu's advice has its own limitations in the sense that it assumes these five traits to be the key traits of leadership and restricts his philosophy.

There are different researches that seek to identify commonalities in leaders. A summary of the identified traits has been given below:

Trait	***Meaning***	***Correlation to Leadership***	***Research/ Researcher***
Extraversion	tendency to be sociable, assertive, active, and to experience positive effects, such as energy and zeal	+ve	Judge and Others (2002)
Agreeableness	tendency to be trusting, compliant, caring, and gentle	+ve	Judge and Others (2002)
Conscientious-ness	it comprises two related facets, namely achievement and dependability and (also keeping organised)	+ve	Judge and Others (2002)
Openness	disposition to be imaginative, non-conforming, unconventional, and autonomous.	+ve	Judge and Others (2002)
Neuroticism	represents the tendency to exhibit poor emotional adjustment and experience negative effects, such as anxiety, insecurity, and hostility	-ve	Judge and Others (2002)
Honesty/ integrity	being truthful and non-deceitful	+ve	Locke, 1991; Hoffman et al., 2011
Charisma	Charismatic leaders are able to influence followers by	+ve	Hoffman et al., 2011

	articulating a compelling vision for the future, arousing commitment to organisational objectives and inspiring commitment and a sense of self-efficacy among followers		
Intelligence	Cognitive and problem solving ability	+ve	Judge et al., 2004
Creativity	Incremental creativity (the ability to come up with novel ideas based on an already available idea) and out-of-the-box thinking	+ve	Hoffman et al., 2011
Achievement motivation	Motivation to gain more resources accolades	+ve	Judge et al., 2002
Need for power	Characterised by the satisfaction leaders derive from exerting influence over the attitudes and behaviours of others	+ve	McClelland &Boyatzis, 1982
Oral/written communication	The clarity and incisiveness displayed in communicating	+ve 2011	Hoffman et al.,
Interpersonal skills	broad range of skills associated with an understanding of human behaviour and the dynamics of groups	+ve	Locke, 1991; Yukl, 2006; Hoffman et al., 2011
General problem solving	Ability to come up with solutions while working with constraints	+ve	Hoffman et al., 2011

Decision making	The ability to evaluate circumstances, future outcomes and to take decisions	+ve	Hoffman et al., 2011
Technical knowledge	Knowledge of methods, processes, and equipment for conducting the specialised activities of the managers' organisational unit	+ve	Bass, 1990
Management skills	Skills like planning, organising, staffing, controlling, directing etc.	+ve	Hoffman et al., 2011

Another interesting research in this regard has been discussed by Professor Alen Skid in a London School of Economics open lecture (also available as a podcast) on the question – "What makes a National Icon?" According to Skid's study of the life history of national icons such as Winston Churchill, Abraham Lincoln, Napoleon Bonaparte and others, three common points have emerged:

- Death and martyrdom
- Participation in War/National Struggle (and victory)
- National icons are expected to be progressive

His other observations about these leaders are as follows:

- They worked hard.
- They combined the role of civil and military leaders
- Didn't have to worry much about opposition.
- All were probably atheists.
- All had an ambiguous sex life.
- Contemplated/ attempted suicide.
- Wars that they were involved in, were largely of their own making.

- Results of their career – millions of ordinary people died!
- Dictated almost everything, especially in matters of war.

Skid eventually concluded that these leaders were not really national leaders and may be the world would have been a better place without them.

The writer of this essay has disagreements with Skid's observations, yet the merit in Skid's thought is an acknowledgement of the fact that not only traits but situational factors have influenced and have been influenced by leaders. Hence, one of the jobs of leaders is to influence situations and also mould themselves as per the situations.

The theories that hold that different situations demand different types of leaders but leaders who are fit for a particular situation cannot be developed to fit into leadership positions called upon by new situations are partially correct. However, where they go wrong is that they completely overlook historical examples when the same sets of leaders have been able to redefine themselves and have been able to succeed in different situations. Examples in this regard are leaders like Nelson Mandela who on the one hand been able to build and lead military organisations such as MK (Umkhonto-we-Sizwe) have also been able to lead democratic and peaceful governments successfully.

Those theories that hold that different situations demand different types of leaders and the same leaders can be developed to lead in different kinds of situations seem true since the most successful leaders are those who have constantly redefined themselves and have stood the test of time. These include Gandhi, Nehru, Nelson Mandela even Lenin. A situational theory forwarded by some researchers is of this spirit. It is the one that argues that a more authoritative or centralised form of a leadership is best suited in situations of high pressure/uncertainty as well as in those of extremely low pressure/uncertainty; and a more relaxed form of a leadership is best suited in situations of moderate pressure/uncertainty.

A casual experiment

The abovementioned theory got me along with some classmates of mine involved in a casual experiment that produced surprising results.

The theory was partially adopted –

"that a more authoritative or centralised form of a leadership is best suited in situations of high pressure/uncertainty and a more relaxed form of a leadership is best suited in situations of moderate pressure/uncertainty as opposed to adopting an authoritative leadership style throughout irrespective of the situation".

We had recently founded a social science society by the name of Vichaar in our MBA institute. One of the primary activities of the society was to organise a debate competition in which groups of nine members would debate against each other. The selection of debaters in the two groups was on the basis of application which included one question to check creative thinking – such as "What is your suggestion for a tagline for the Vichaar Committee?" or "How would you handle such and such situation?"; and another question would have to be selected from among a set of questions that sought the applicant's opinion on a particular social issue. After receiving the application casual interactions were conducted with the applicants to judge them on the following parameters:

- Confidence in Public Speaking
- Fluency in English

It was the philosophy of Vichaar to not only restrict participation to those who were already skilled in the art of public speaking. Rather its philosophy was to develop public speaking skills and a sense of socio-political awareness in everyone as Vichaar held these to be some of the essential managerial and leadership competencies. Hence, each team was selected in a manner so as to have an equal distribution of those who are adept in public speaking and those who were still comparatively, lightweights. A committee two teams of nine shortlisted candidates each was formed based on the abovementioned considerations. Each team was allotted two mentors each from the

Vichaar Committee to guide them through the debating format and also to prepare the respective teams for some serious debating.

The topic for the debate was:

"This house believes that India needs a dictatorial government to prosper"

Finally, a time of five to seven days was given for both the teams to prepare with their mentors.

Now as we had decided, one set of mentors assumed a more centralised form of a leadership style throughout the preparation period–by themselves allocating the captain and vice-captain of their team, by defining the order of speaking among the team members and by even now and then writing arguments for the team (in the first debate such mentors were allocated to the side supporting the motion).

The other set of mentors assumed a more situational leadership style (in the first debate such mentors were allocated to the side opposing the motion). That is to say, initially when there was extreme discomfort in the team regarding the new debating format and with regards to public speaking the mentors would help the team, train them by making them speak in front of the camera, and by making them do a lot of uncomfortable stuff such as addressing a party gathering etc.; even helping them in their arguments here and there (I happened to be the mentor of this team the first time), while refraining themselves from appointing positions such as the president, researchers etc. and only making slight suggestions or not making any suggestions at all regarding the order of speaking. However, once the team got more and more used to the format and the idea of debating and public speaking sunk in (which happened after 2-3 days of preparation), the mentors withdrew their support gradually and just before the last one or two days of the debate even stopped meeting their teams. One night before the actual event a 'grilling session' was conducted for both the teams separately, one by one, wherein the committee members and the speaker for the house listened to the arguments of the respective teams and cross questioned them so as to challenge their arguments. This was done to create a pressure situation for both the teams and also to gauge the sophistication of arguments prepared by both the teams. No scores were assigned for this stage.

There was always a divide among the committee mentors on as to which team would perform better on the D-day after going about the "grilling sessions". However, two committee members were asked to take a 'temperature check' of the two teams to gauge their level of confidence after the "grilling session". The mentors of the respective teams accompanied the non-mentoring committee members for the 'temperature checks' and would engage the participants in conversation asking about how they think they had performed. Invariably the team that had an authoritative mentor reported that they felt self-assured and were hopeful to win the debate the next day. Also invariably the team that had the situational leadership style mentors reported they felt they did not perform too well and that they need another rigorous round of preparation.

At this juncture, the mentor of the latter team again got involved in the preparation for D-day. The authoritative mentors too were with their team for the preparation of D-day (they basically had the reigns in their hands from the beginning till the end). Practices almost always went on till late in the night before the day of the final debate.

The final debate was arranged in the slot of 3:00 pm to 4:00 pm or 3:30 pm to 4:30 pm every time so that participants got enough sleep and sufficient time after lunch to relax.

The debate was judged in two manners –

1. By an independent judge who would either be a leading journalist, a professor, politician or a leading professional in the field related to the subject. (In this case it was a professor both the times)
2. By the audience

The audience was also asked to cast their opinion poll once before the debate and cast their final judgment at the end of the debate.

Surprisingly, in the first debate, the side with the situational leadership style mentor won the vote of the audience and the judge as well!

The experiment with the same topic was repeated a second time. New teams were formed, only the mentors were interchanged that is the set of mentors following the authoritative style were allocated to the team opposing the motion, while the mentors who adopted the situational leadership style were allocated to the group supporting the motion.

Similar situations recurred. The team with the authoritative mentors reported a higher sense of confidence after the "grilling session" as compared to the other team. And as had happened before, the team with the situational leadership mentors again won both the audience votes as well as the judge's.

The same set of experiments was repeated with a second topic:

"This house believes that the state of Bihar is the next powerhouse of India's economic growth"

This also returned similar results.

A third set of experiment was again conducted with the topic:

"This house believes that prostitution should be legalised in India"

Again the situational style won both the time (although by a close margin in the second experiment in terms of audience vote; the judge in the second round refused to pass any judgment).

These experiments were conducted in forms of debates in the year of 2013, however, due to the busy schedule of B-school the Vichaar team was not able to compile and publish the findings and as Vichaar expanded its areas of operations, recruited new members and organised new events the research was relegated into the back of the minds of all the committee members. Finally, with great pleasure I submit hereby, the conclusions of the series of experiments that was the result of a discussion after the first few debates, as follows:

- That a more authoritative or centralised form of a leadership is best suited in situations of high pressure/uncertainty and a more relaxed form of a leadership is best suited in situations of moderate pressure/uncertainty as opposed to adopting an authoritative leadership style throughout irrespective of the situation.

- That groups under the leadership of those who are authoritative and who micro-manage throughout are more confident of their victory (this sounds a little similar to Germany's confidence in their victory during the Second World War.)
- That the groups under the leader with a situational leadership style perform better than groups working under leaders who constantly centralise power and micromanage.
- While coordinating availability for practice sessions used to be a challenge for both groups, the groups working under the leader with a situational leadership style would become self-organised and would coordinate practice sessions by themselves soon after the leaders would reduce their own involvement.
- A second rung of leadership would also emerge in groups working under the leader with a situational leadership style, however not without initial conflicts. These conflicts had indeed been resolved by the mentor a lot of times. In fact, in one of the debates there was a conflict about who will be the opening speaker. I was the mentor of that group and had assumed the situational leadership style. However, as the team was not able to resolve the issue by itself, I intervened and nominated one of the two conflicting members for the position of the first speaker. The other candidate for speaker position, in the celebration party post victory in the debate (a party that took place nearly 15 days after the victory) still passed on a friendly complaint that he could still not understand why he was not allowed to be the opening speaker. I only said that I thought he would be much more valuable in the rebuttal rounds and had wanted him to concentrate on the rebuttal more than the opening statements.

- There would always be two to three people in each group who would be comparatively lesser willing to come for the practice sessions.They would be kept under check by the authoritative leader at all times (one such person was also asked to leave the team by one of the super-authoritative leaders). In case of the situational leadership style led team such people would only propel into action after the "grilling sessions".

Further scope of research:

- Experiments including a third group led by a laissez faire style of leadership in the current set of experiments may reveal new aspects about the nature and results of different leadership styles.
- Greater clarity on how much authority and how much leniency might a leader adopt while opting for a situational style of leadership can add more value to the current findings.
- Creation of excessively easy situations of certainty after tough and moderate situations of uncertainty might reveal if a more authoritative leadership style also suits best to easy and stable situations. This can be done by repeating the group composition and changing debate topics. The assumption being that the victorious group may become complacent.
- To find reasons why the state of shock (in the grilling session) leads the group with the situational leaders to overtake the other group and to find whether they will still overtake the other group in final preparation and performance even if their leaders do not again participate with the group and choose not to intervene even after the situation of shock.
- To judge the performance of both the groups if they are told that the grilling session will also be marked and the marks shall be added to the final score.

- To swap members and/or mentors midway and evaluate results.
- To have groups of different competence level compete under different leadership styles and thereby evaluate results.

Implications

- The best style of leadership is perhaps not to have a constant style but to fluctuate smoothly.
- The ability to change one's leadership style and that of redefining oneself has perhaps led leaders like Gandhi, Mandela and Lenin to make their movements a success (as has been discussed in the case studies below).

Case Analysis: A case study of Gandhi's Leadership and the Causes of Success of the Gandhian Movement

"I saw him (first) in 1918-1919 when I was a student of University School of Law. They were discussing the Congress Pledge. Motilal Nehru was there. Gandhi stood up and slapped himself in the face. Next I saw him in Kanpur where Benarsidas arranged, so to say, an interview with him. Bapu Hazarilal and some of us went. It was Friday, Maun-divas (the day of observing silence by Gandhi). Miss Sledge was sitting beside him (Gandhi). He answered the questions by writing on a slate. Finally, I saw him at Firozabad during his whirlwind tour in 1930. R.N. Tandon was with him. I presented him a short address...To write anything about this world famous man or his activities to drive away British Raj or people acting as one body or NATION is not possible in a short note..."

— Diary entry of Pt. Sushil Chandra Chaturvedi (5/8/1979)

The above is a diary entry of my great grandfather who remembered his meetings with Gandhiji fondly. The impact of Mohandas Karamchand Gandhi was immense on anybody who happened to meet him. In fact, having the magnitude of impact that Gandhi had on such a huge proportion of population of the world is something perhaps unachieved by any other leader in history. Gandhi's leadership style is a case study of a leader who adapted to circumstances and changed circumstances in his own turn. He was able to bring people together – one of the largest and most diverse set of population in the world, get their ideas aligned while he changed leadership style as per the situation's demands.

There are diverse opinions about Gandhi and his leadership style. The plethora of diverse opinions about Gandhi is most interesting for understanding how a person can influence the course of history.

The journey of Mohandas Karamchand Gandhi began in India with the Champaran Struggle. The nationalist movement in India before the arrival of Gandhi from South Africa has been described by Judith Brown as a "politics of studies limitation" and by Ravinder Kumar as a "movement representing the classes as opposed to the masses" participated only by a limited group of western educated professionals. In the words of Jawaharlal Nehru "Gandhi came like a powerful whirlwind of fresh air, like a beam of light, like a whirlwind."

External Factors that Prepared the Stage for Gandhi

Many historians have stressed on the role of external factors to the rise of Gandhi. Price rise, inflation owing to the war, increase in defence expenditure, transport bottlenecks and food shortages have been furnished as reasons for converting India into a ripe ground for political action a scenario which suitably synchronised with the time of Gandhi's entry into the Indian National Movement. Other historians have also pointed out that the loss of Russia at the hands of the Japanese in the Russo-Japanese War helped in shattering the invincibility of western imperialism in the eyes of Asia. At the same time, a new confidence was created by the success of global political movements such as the Russian Revolution.

The First World War, depression and the Second World War brought about significant changes in the structure of colonial exploitation stimulating political action by combining new grievances with growing strength. One of the major developments of the First World War was the market capture by the indigenous industries of India due to the shift in production of the English industries to arms and ammunitions. This resulted in the assertion of power by the Indian industrialists and even the workers. Once the world war was over and the trade bottlenecks created by the war cleared, the hike in demand for Indian production dissipated. By now the Indian business class grew more confident and was ready to voice their grievances and disagreements. De-industrialisation and declining wages after the First World War initiated the joining of hands of the conflicting classes to create a movement. Hence a political ground for agitation was created in a commercial sector.

As per Blyn's findings, the demographic growth in the "greater Bengal region" (i.e. modern day Bengal, Assam, Bihar, and parts of Odisha) led to an actual decline in the per capita foodgrain output in that region (thereby preparing this area as a hotbed of political activities as a result of grievances owing to food and material shortage). Stephen Henningham has shown that acceleration in population growth in Northern Bihar contributed to the transformation of "an isolated backwater to a centre of militant agrarian and political movements". David Hardiman in his study of Kheda during early 1930s has shown that economic determinism in the region was still enormous. The shortage of food and growth of population led to the radicalisation of peasantry.

Hence, many historians believe that the post war economic changes and demographic growth in certain parts of India created a fertile situation for a big political movement to take shape. Such a movement, as per some historians, was more of the creation of demographic, economic and international political factors and not of Gandhi.

However, to argue that the question of socio-economic conjectures was the sole reason for the rise of Gandhi would fail to explain why didn't any person other than Gandhi appear on the political forefront leading the movement which had already been allegedly created by external forces; or why didn't such a movement against colonial rule begin in any other post First World War British colony. The basic assumption, behind much economic determinism, argues Sarkar, is that growing misery is a sufficient explanation of popular action which is extremely dubious and begs the whole question as to what kinds of socio-economic situations where most conductive to Gandhian or Non-Gandhian mass movements. As George Lefebvre has rightly pointed out that the "true causal link between social, economic or political causes and the event or (its) effects has to be sought in the formation of specific collective frames of mind". And it is in terms of crucial shifts in the collective frames of mind that it is best to try to understand the phenomenon of Gandhi. He was also helped, argues Sarkar, somewhat fortuitously by his South African example to gain a world reputation and also the possibility of contacts cutting across regions, communities and classes in a manner which was unthinkable for any other Indian politician of the early twentieth century and yet it is difficult to ignore the millennial aspect of Gandhi's mass appeal.

External Factors-Internal Leadership: Gandhi's Situational Leadership Style

Gandhi's leadership style combined the forces of external realities with effective management[1] of ideas, people and events. Gandhi had perhaps understood what Tolstoy enunciated in his epic War and Peace– "To abandon the conception of cause …and to seek law"[2]. In the sense that he understood that a combination of the right ideas, events and people in interplay with the existing situation, would be the only course of achieving the desired goal of independence – although he may not have been sure himself that he would see Independence during his lifetime. Gandhi's prime quality lies in combining paradoxes to create a positive unitary force as has been shown in the following sections. The second greatest achievement of Gandhi is perhaps not to bring a vast number of people together in a movement, but to kindle a spirit in the peoples of the nation that it could, as it were in its current state, with its current capabilities, loom over the British Raj and win freedom. Here again Tolstoy's words may have influenced him "That unknown quantity is the spirit of the army, that is to say, the greater or lesser readiness to fight and face danger felt by all the men composing an army… The spirit of an army is the factor which multiplied by the mass gives the resulting force…."[3] Gandhi's prime achievement was to invoke a spirit in every citizen of the nation to drive off the imperialists from their country.

Managing Ideas

Gandhi was a virtuoso at managing ideas and he did not do so by forcing his ideas on others, but by reiterating ideas that his audience held so dearly in a manner to suit his subject. In the words of Jawaharlal Nehru "He (Gandhi) did not descend from the top; he seemed to emerge from the millions of Indians, speaking their language and incessantly drawing attention to them and their appalling conditions." Some historians believe likewise that his way of dressing, his language, his whole way of living were ways to relate himself with the masses of the nation. Travelling third class, speaking in simple Hindustani, wearing only loin-cloth from 1921 onwards, and using the imagery of Tulsidas's Ramayana, Gandhi was able to establish a connect with the self-perceived identities of the masses.

According to A.L. Basham "Gandhi was fully aware of Indian pluralism and took care not to alienate any of the communities or classes. He agreed that (his) ideology must be rooted in India and its ancient civilisation. He successfully used religious idioms to mobilise the masses". His continuous use of Rama Rajya and other religious characters lent him the essential mass-connect as per Basham. "His early exposure to Vaishnavism and Jainism in Gujrat influenced him" (Basham). His readings of western thinkers like Henry David Thoreau, John Ruskin, Leo Tolstoy etc. inspired his ideas and gave him a global appeal.

For Partha Chatterjee, his philosophy represented a "Critique of Civil Society" or to put it more directly – "a fundamental critique of the entire edifice of bourgeois society". Manfred Steger has called it a "critique of liberalism"; while for Bhikhu Parekh his ideology was a "critique of modern civilisation". On the other hand, others such as Anthony Parel thought of Gandhi as essentially modern in his thought. His stress on women liberation, his later arguments for inter-religion and inter-caste marriages and dining, and his insistence on performing manual, even menial work – all reflected a sense of modernity in its essence. It was perhaps this mixture of opposites that lent a particular enigma and charisma to Gandhi's persona and added to his appeal. In final analysis we can say that Gandhi was able to manage ideas by borrowing from different ideological traditions and synthesising his own interpretations of such ideas.

Managing People

Judith Brown has tried to explain Gandhi's rise to power in terms of skilful political manipulation through "sub-contractors". According to Sarkar, "it is perfectly true that the Mahatma combined a saintly idiom and apparent quixotry with meticulous and extremely able attention to organisational details".

However, Gandhi in my opinion fitted perfectly in the description of a transformational leader and demonstrated the following four features of transformational leadership that was the base of his referent power:

At the same time Gandhi was also a transactional leader. Transactional leadership establishes and standardises practices that

Leadership Attribute	*Meaning*	*Gandhi's Practice*
Idealised Influence (II)	The leader serves as an ideal role model for followers; the leader "walks the talk," and is admired for this	Remember the Dandi March? Noakhali, Champaran, South Africa? Living in London slums during the round table conference, living an ascetic life (despite hailing from an affluent background) Need one say more?
Inspirational Motivation (IM)	Transformational leaders have the ability to inspire and motivate followers.	Gandhi's inspirational speeches, prayer meetings.
Individualised Consideration (IC)	Transformational leaders demonstrate genuine concern for the needs and feelings of followers. This personal attention to each follower is a key element in bringing out their very best efforts.	Innumerable letters written by Gandhi to his colleagues from different walks of life are a proof.
Intellectual Stimulation (IS)	Leaders challenge followers to be innovative and creative. They also open new perspectives of thought and introduce followers to new ideas.	His book: My Experiments with Truth

help the organisation reach maturity, emphasising setting of goals, efficiency of operation, and increase of productivity. His adherence to strict routines at his Ashrams, his readiness to even punish (at times even comrades in arms) through fasting, hard negotiations at the round table conferences point towards the versatility of his leadership style without attaching a specific attachment to any one style.

Managing Events

A mixture of opposites also culminated in Gandhi's mode of Protest–Satyagraha. Indian politicians before Gandhi tended to oscillate between "moderate mendicancy and individual terrorism" opined a historian. The Satyagraha concept of controlled yet vigorous mass participation now offered a way out of the impasse. Some historians say that non-violence attracted mass participation and conflicting sections of the society without disturbing its equilibrium (earlier there were examples of movements being dissipated because of the exacerbation of internal conflicts of the protesting side). Gandhi's movement was an umbrella struggle where anybody could join with minimum risk of internecine conflict with the Gandhian idea of non-violence. It was a movement where everybody had a reason to join, according to Sumit Sarkar—the bourgeoisie looked forward to better opportunities, working classes too looked forward to better terms of employment and higher wages, peasants expected freedom to grow what they wanted and women had liberation to look forward to. Moreover, the movement owing to its non-violent nature, would also last longer because of its marginal chances to attract violent retaliation.

Nevertheless, the Non-Cooperation movement did get violent and after the Chauri-Chaura incidence, when Gandhi as a method of negative reinforcement and to reiterate a commitment to non-violence withdrew the initiative, many accused him of betrayal. Even fellow comrades such as Motilal Nehru, C.R. Das, Jawaharlal Nehru, Subhash Chandra Bose and many others have noted and expressed their utter bewilderment on why the whole nation had to pay the price for the outrageous behaviour of some of the people in a remote village. R. Palme Dutt in his 'India Today' and many other later commentators have gone as far as condemning the decision taken by Mahatma Gandhi construing the same as a proof of the Mahatma's concern for the propertied classes of the Indian society. According to Dutt, the reformist-pacifist control over the movement was indeed weakening but the movement in terms of its effective strength was only getting stronger. Dutt highlights the fact by quoting a government report of three days before the withdrawal that suggests that the movement was a disorder of a formidable nature. According to Dutt, the phraseology of 'non-violence' was only a cover, conscious or unconscious of class interests, but for the maintenance of class exploitation. The Marxists overall have accused Gandhi for getting frightened of growing radicalisation and the fact that radical forces would take over the reins of the movement and may thereby hurt the interests of the capitalists and the propertied class. The problem however, with this argument is the interchangeable use of the word violence for radicalisation– which in reality denotes different meanings –violence is not concomitant to radicalisation and vice-versa.

Similarly, the Subaltern School charges Gandhi of not letting the movement go out of his hands. The Subaltern School talks of "Gandhian breaks" which were applied to the national movement whenever the equilibrium of the society seemed to be getting disturbed.

It seems that Gandhi's critics have been less than fair to him. In fact, some politicians such as Nelson Mandela[4] as well as a few Indian historians such as Bipan Chandra have seen non-violence as more of a strategy than anything else. Violence could initiate a violent reaction to suppress the movement and Gandhi knew very well that if the movement got crushed, a wave of demoralisation would envelope the nation. "True that the withdrawal itself caused demoralisation" opines Bipan Chandra, but the movement was to re-emerge in 1930 as the Civil Disobedience Movement. Bipan Chandra goes further to claim that Chauri-chaura can hardly be taken as a sign of radicalisation of the movement as at Chauri-chaura there was no intention on part of those who burned the 22 policemen, to outrage or overthrow the landlords and it was a mere reaction to the violent behaviour of the policemen.

In fact it seems completely plausible and wise that in a battle among unequal powers using the same tools (i.e. violence and suppression) to fight a superior force would have been devastating and hence, a separate strategy of warfare had to be innovated and this strategy for Gandhi was Satyagraha and Ahinsa. This was also perhaps the result of Gandhi's analysis of the nature and state of the British colonial rule at that stage of history and his experiments in understanding the nature of the Raj successfully conducted in South Africa would have come in handy.

Bipan Chandra stressing on the strategic nature of the Gandhian movement has argued that "mass movement have an inherent tendency to ebb after reaching a certain height... that the capacity of the masses to withstand repression, endure sufferings and make sacrifices is not unlimited...that a time comes when breathing space is required to consolidate, recuperate and gather strength for the next round of struggle and ...therefore withdrawal is not tantamount to betrayal, it is the inevitable part of the strategy itself." According to Chandra "Gandhiji perhaps had enough reasons for this controversial move (of withdrawing the Non-Cooperation movement)". The movement had already gone already for an year, the government was in no mind for negotiations and Chauri-chaura presented an opportunity for retreat with honour before the internal weaknesses of the movement became apparent enough to force a surrender or make the retreat look like a rout (Bipan Chandra).

According to Bipan Chandra, Gandhiji followed a strategy of Struggle-Truce-Struggle (S-T-S), wherein a period of struggle would be followed by a period of truce and it would be in this period of truce that Gandhi would replenish the lost energy of the masses, taking time out in his Ashrams to educate people and consolidate them. Once a sufficient degree of energy was regained, Gandhi launched the second phase of struggle in form of the Civil Disobedience Movement and finally the Quit India Movement when he gave the slogan "do or die". In the words of Sumit Sarkar, "here also lay the paradox of Gandhian politics, for he wanted not just any mass upsurge, but a controlled mass movement which could adhere to his prescribed path". Hence, Gandhi was also able to manage events with a skill that is no short of being exemplary.

Conclusion

Hence, looking at Gandhi's example it seems that leadership seems to operate on three different levels –

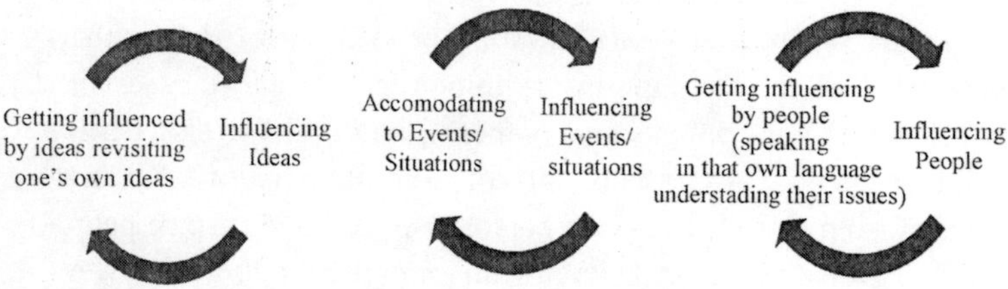

And, the key to success for leaders is to –

1. Bring people together
2. Get their ideas aligned
3. Change leadership style as per the demand of the situation

There are many examples to learn from but the philosophy of leadership in its essence relates to the aspects discussed above. While history may provide different examples to different people, the philosophy remains essentially the same since "History is philosophy taught by example". Indeed Gandhi was not the perfect controller and it was perhaps not his intention to be, as it is not for any leader. There were times when for Gandhi things got out of control in terms of ideas, events and people. In terms of ideas, Sumit Sarkar has discussed about rumours resulting from faith in Gandhi (which of course were not an intended effect of Gandhi's ideology)—Santhals attacked the police in Jalpaiguri in February 1922 wearing Gandhian caps which they claimed made them "immune to bullets". In the realm of events the Non-Cooperation movement indeed did go out of hands. As far as people are concerned, Gandhi did lose, to an extent, erstwhile supporters such as Subhash Chandra Bose and many others. But

Gandhi perhaps had the ability to learn, stumble and quickly get up again, to make the best out of the worst situations to plan like a general and to inspire like a sage, he had a moral strength, patience to wait, build momentum and an instinct to seize opportunity when it presented itself. All this led Gandhi to manage the course of history as best as one could. The challenge in front of him was to combine weak, disparate, unequal and conflicting groups together against a strong and united force and through his balance, incessant efforts and will he was able to overcome the challenges and emerge victorious.

In fact, we can argue that Gandhi was able to bring all the three Cs together—**Common Goal** (Swaraj and ousting of the British), **Contact** (of hitherto competing religions, castes and classes in a controlled and non-violent environment), and (re) **Categorisation** (of all these people as "Indians" striving to build a nation). What we also learn from Gandhi is how a person can lead and inspire people to join the group +ve, despite having an immense amount of power – even a celebrity status – among people. In final observation, what we can learn from Gandhi is that leadership is not a one-dimensional and undirectional function but it is to be altered, transformed and redefined by developing a keen consciousness of the situation and a will to push forward one way or the other as per the allowance of circumstances – only to change them.

References

1. Management here is not tantamount to manipulation as many argue about Gandhi without understanding his politics properly.
2. See Second Epilogue War and Peace by Leo Tolstoy. Translated by Louise and Aylmer Maude.
3. *Ibid.*
4. See generally "Long Walk to Freedom: The Autobiography of Nelson Mandela" and Mandela: The Authorised Biography by Anthony Sampson.

APPENDIX

Perspective Taking—A take on the Formulation of International Laws

By Upasana Singh and Arpit Chaturvedi

Introduction

> *We stand today at the threshold of great event, both in the light of the United Nations and in the light of the mankind. This Universal Declaration of Human Rights may well become the international Magna Carta of all men everywhere.*
>
> Eleanor Roosevelt[1]

More than half a century has passed since 10 December 1948, the day United Nations General Assembly (UNGA) adopted the Universal Declaration of Human Rights (UDHR). In the aftermath of the Second World War, it was the first attempt towards establishing certain norms, values and principles which would be respected and guaranteed across the globe. Determining the source of international human rights law can be just as controversial as defining its content, with various stakeholders asserting different philosophical, moral, and empirical perspectives to support or refute the abundant legal theories on the matter. One of the most intellectually rich tensions in this debate is that between the universal theory of human rights and the theory of cultural relativism, and a great deal of scholarship has been dedicated to solving the conflict between the two.

This essay deals with the origin and meaning of human rights as perceived by the world. Dealing particularly with the cross-cultural aspect of the debate an attempt has been made to show that the real bone of contention is not the general acceptance to the idea that human rights are the basic rights of every human of every society or culture; but the mechanism for setting the standards for deciding as to what constitutes human rights. For avoiding discussions in the abstract and to arrive at a clearer picture the essay deals with a case study on the basic agenda of human rights advocates of today – the protection of individual against cruel, inhuman, and degrading treatment and punishment. This is not an attempt to side with any of the views but it is an attempt to discover the real cause of the conflict.

Origin of Human Rights

Human rights cover thousands of years and draws upon religious, cultural, philosophical and legal developments throughout the recorded history. However, prior to World War II, the importance of human rights was not much recognised. The heinous crimes and killings committed during the war left a permanent scar in the minds of the people. The problem could neither be dealt with utilitarianism, scientific positivism nor philosophies. After the war, the Nuremberg War Crimes Tribunal introduced the subject of gross human rights violations to the international relation. In effect, it can be said that the concept of human rights strengthened in reaction to the horrors of war.[2]

Human rights are inherent inalienable right that is granted to us by virtue of being born as a human being. Various approaches to human rights have been developed over the years[3]:

1. The natural law approach, based on equality, have contemplated that natural law should be given the highest priority and positive law should be subordinate to it.
2. The historical approach views law as a product of the national culture, embedded in the daily practices of the people; law begins as culture and ends as the law of the state.

3. The positivist approach sees law "as enacted by authoritarian sovereign deriving sanctions from coercion".
4. Marxist approach is of the view that human rights exist only in classless society where there is public ownership of the means of production.
5. The Social Science approach views that human rights are in a large context of social processes, dwelling on the community's role in shaping principles.

Among the various approach to human rights, the natural law theory gained much importance in the historical development of human rights. Greeks were the first profounder of natural law theory. In Greek period, the concept of human rights held a greater meaning than the prevention of arbitrary prosecution and recognised universal law for all mankind under which all men are equal. According to Socrates and Plato, natural law is the law that reflects the natural order of the universe. Human rights were further promoted in the medieval age. St. Thomas Aquinas, in an attempt to harmonise the teachings of the church with those of natural law, observed that law of nature is the discovery of eternal law through reason and reason is the main manifestation of religion[4].

Meaning of Human Rights

Human rights thus came to be evolved as those of the natural rights which are fundamental to the very existence and growth of a human being and which every civilized society would like to ensure unto them, albeit in its own larger interest[5]. Therefore, it can be said that the rights that all people have by virtue of their being human are human rights. These are the rights which no one can be deprived without a grave affront to justice[6].

Donnelly defines human rights as "inalienable entitlements of individuals held against the state and the society" simply because they are human beings.[7]

D.D. Basu defines human rights as those minimum rights which every individual must have against the State or other public authority by virtue of his being a member of human family, irrespective of any other consideration.[8]

According to Bennet "*Human rights include those areas of individual or group freedom that are immune from governmental interference or that, because of their basic contribution to human dignity or welfare, are subject to governmental guarantee, protections or promotion*".[9]

Evolution of Legal Documents

The **Magna Carta** was signed in June 1215 between the barons and King John. 'Magna Carta' in Latin means "Great Charter". The Magna Carta was one of the most important documents of Medieval England. Magna Carta was an attempt by the barons to prevent a king from abusing his power and cause suffering for the people of England.

The Magna Carta enumerates what later came to be thought of as human rights. Among them was the right of the Church to be free from governmental interference, the right of all free citizens to own and inherit property and to be protected from excessive taxes[10]. It established the rights of widows to owned properties, to choose not to remarry, and established principles of due process and equality before the law. It also contained provisions forbidding bribery and official misconduct.

Among the most important rules of the Magna Carta that we still use today is the writ of *habeas corpus*, which means "Do you have the body?" in Latin[11]. This rule means that the government can't arrest people without cause or in secret and guarantees the right to due process. If it was not for the Magna Carta, the laws around the world would be completely different today. Without the Magna Carta, there would be no United States Constitution or a Universal Declaration of Human Rights.

The Bill of Rights, 1689, is an Act of the Parliament of England passed on 16 December 1689. It was a restatement in statutory form of the Declaration of Right presented by the Convention Parliament to William and Mary in March 1689 (or 1688 by Old Style dating), inviting them to become joint sovereigns of England[12]. It lays down limits on the powers of the crown and sets out the rights of Parliament and rules for freedom of speech in Parliament, the requirement for regular elections to Parliament and the right to petition the monarch without fear of retribution.

French Declaration of the Right of Man and of the Citizen 1789 was introduced by a preamble describing the fundamental characteristics of the rights which are qualified as being "natural, unalienable and sacred" and consisting of "simple and incontestable principles" on which citizens could base their demands. In the second article, "the natural and imprescriptible rights of man" are defined as "liberty, property, security and resistance to oppression"[13]. It called for the destruction of aristocratic privileges by proclaiming an end to exemptions from taxation, freedom and equal rights for all human beings (referred to as "Men"), and access to public office based on talent. The monarchy was restricted, and all citizens were to have the right to take part in the legislative process. Freedom of speech and press were declared, and arbitrary arrests outlawed.

The Bill of Rights 1791 is the collective name for the first ten amendments to the United States Constitution. Proposed to assuage the fears of Anti-Federalists who had opposed Constitutional ratification, these amendments guarantee a number of personal freedoms, limit the government's power in judicial and other proceedings, and reserve some powers for the states and the public[14]. The amendments were introduced by James Madison to the 1st United States Congress as a series of legislative articles. The Bill of Rights is a list of limits on government power.

Development of International Institutions

The idea of human rights emerged stronger after World War II. The extermination by Nazi Germany of over six million Jews, Sinti and Romani (gypsies), homosexuals and persons with disabilities horrified the world. Thus, human rights became a matter of international concern with the end of World War II which invariably led to the formulation of the United Nations[15]. Since then, the international human rights law has been developing in an unprecedented way and has become a very substantive part of international law as a whole.

One of the most significant repercussions of the World War II was the formulation of a world body—**"United Nations"** replacing the League of Nations which was widely considered to have been ineffective in its role as an international governing body, as it had been unable to prevent World War II. The UN was an international organisation whose stated aims were to facilitate cooperation in international law, international security, economic development, social progress, human rights and achieving world peace. As the UN Code, the United Nations Charter was drafted which was perhaps one the most important steps put forward by the states worldwide towards protection and preservation of human rights. It was the United Nations that led to the drafting of various documents towards protection of human rights such as Universal Declaration of Human Rights, International Covenant on Civil and Political Rights, International Covenant on Economic, Social and Cultural Rights, the Genocide Convention, etc.

On December 10, 1948, the **Universal Declaration of Human Rights (UDHR)**was adopted by the 56 members of the United Nations. The UDHR extended the revolution in international law ushered in by the United Nations Charter–namely, that how a government treats its own citizens is now a matter of legitimate international concern, and not simply a domestic issue[16]. The Universal Declaration is often considered the foundation stone for modern human rights. Since the Declaration was adopted in 1948 it has inspired over 80 international conventions and treaties, as well as numerous regional and domestic conventions, bills and legislation.

With the goal of establishing mechanisms for enforcing the UDHR, the UN Commission on Human Rights proceeded to draft two *treaties*: the International Covenant on Civil and Political Rights **(ICCPR)** and its optional *Protocol* and the International Covenant on Economic, Social and Cultural Rights **(ICESCR).** Together with the Universal Declaration, they are commonly referred to as the *International Bill of Human Rights*. The ICCPR focuses on such issues as the right to life, freedom of speech, religion, and voting. The ICESCR focuses on such issues as food, education, health, and shelter. Both *covenants* trumpet the extension of rights to all persons and prohibit discrimination[17].

Universalism and Cultural Relativism

There are two dominant arguments about the sources of Human Rights:

1. Universalism, the theory that Human Rights are universal and inure to the person by virtue of his or her personal hood and
2. Cultural Relativism, the theory that Human Rights, to the extent that they exist at all are relative to one's culture and can only be understood or enforced by the members of that culture.

The question of the 'universal' or 'relative' character of rights declared in the major instruments of human rights movement has been a source of debate and contention from the movement's start. Cultural relativism is the view that all beliefs, customs, and ethics are relative to the individual within his own social context. In other words, "right" and "wrong" are culture-specific; what is considered moral in one society may be considered immoral in another, and, since no universal standard of morality exists, no one has the right to judge another society's customs.

- *From Within and Without*

The cultural challenge to the universality of human rights arises from three distinct sources-from resurgent Islam, from within the West itself, and from East Asia. Each of these challenges is independent of the others, but taken together, they have raised substantial questions about the cross-cultural validityand hence the legitimacy of human rights norms.[18]

The challenge from Islam has been there from the beginning. When the Universal Declaration of Human Rights was being drafted in 1947, the Saudi Arabian delegation raised particular objection to

Article 16, relating to free marriage choice, and Article 18, relating to freedom of religion. This was a defence of both the Islamic faith and patriarchal authority.

A second challenge to the universality of human rights comes from within the West itself. For the last 20 years, an influential current in Western political opinion has been maintaining, in the words of the radical scholars Adamantia Poll is and Peter Schwab, that human rights are a "Western construct of limited applicability," a twentieth century fiction dependent on the rights traditions of the United States, the United Kingdom, and France and therefore inapplicable in cultures that do not share this historical matrix of liberal individualism.

This challenge within has been amplified by a challenge from without: the critique of Western human rights standards by some political leaders in the rising economies of East Asia. Whereas, the Islamic challenge to human rights can be explained in part by the failure of Islamic societies to benefit from the global economy, the Asian challenge is a consequence of the region's staggering economic success. Because of Malaysia's robust economic growth, for example, its leaders feel confident enough to reject Western ideas of democracy and individual rights in favour of an Asian route to development and prosperity-a route that depends on authoritarian government and authoritarian family structures.

The same can be said about Singapore, which successfully synthesized political authoritarianism with market capitalism. Singapore's Senior Minister Lee Kuan Yew has been quoted as saying that Asians have "little doubt that a society with communitarian values where the interests of society take precedence over that of the individual suits them better than the individualism of America." Singaporeans often cite rising divorce and crime rates in the West to illustrate that Western individualism is detrimental to the order necessary for the enjoyment of rights themselves.

Let it be conceded at once that these three separate challenges to the universality of human rights discourse-two from without and one from within the Western tradition-have had a productive impact. They have forced human rights activists to question their assumptions, to rethink the history of their commitments, and to realise just how complicated intercultural dialogue on the question of rights becomes when all cultures participate as equals.

- *The Power of One*

Human rights, it is argued, can recover universal appeal only if they soften their individualistic bias and put greater emphasis on the communitarian parts of the declaration, especially Article 29, which says that "everyone has duties to the community in which alone the free and full development of his personality is possible."

But this tack mistakes what rights actually are and misunderstands why they have proven attractive to millions of people raised in non-Western traditions. Rights are meaningful only if they confer entitlements and immunities on individuals; they are worth having only if they can be enforced against institutions such as the family, the state, and the church. This remains true even when the rights in question are collective or group rights.

Rights are inescapably political because they tacitly imply a conflict between a rights holder and a rights "withholder," some authority against which the rights holder can make justified claims. Thus universality cannot imply universal assent, since in a world of unequal power, the only propositions that the powerful and powerless would agree on would be entirely toothless and anodyne. Rights are universal because they define the universal interests of the powerless-namely, that power be exercised over them in ways that respect their autonomy as agents.[19]

- *Cultural Shock*

Adopting the values of individual agency does not necessarily entail adopting Western ways of life. Believing in your right not to be tortured or abused need not mean adopting Western dress, speaking Western languages, or approving of the Western lifestyle. To seek human rights protection is not to change your civilisation; it is merely to avail yourself of the protections of what the philosopher Isaiah Berlin called "negative liberty": to be free from oppression, bondage, and gross physical harm. Human rights do not, and should not, delegitimise traditional culture as a whole. The women in Kabul who come to human rights agencies seeking protection from the Taliban do not want to cease being Muslim wives and mothers; they want to combine their traditions with education and professional health care provided by a woman.

Indeed, what makes human rights demands legitimate is that they emanate from the bottom, from the powerless. Instead of apologising for the individualism of Western human rights standards, activists need to attend to another problem, which is how to create conditions in which individuals on the bottom are free to avail themselves of such rights. The much debated issue of female circumcision illustrates this point. What may appear as mutilation in Western eyes is, in some cultures, simply the price of tribal and family belonging for women. An activist's proper role is not to make the choices for the women in question but to enlarge those women's knowledge of what the choices entail. In traditional societies, harmful practices can be abandoned only when the whole community decides to do so. Otherwise, individuals who decide on their own face ostracism and worse. Consent in these cases means collective or group consent. Yet even group consent must be built on consultation with the individuals involved.

Sensitivity to the real constraints that limit individual freedom in different cultures is not the same thing as deferring to these cultures. It does not mean abandoning universality. It simply means facing up to a demanding intercultural dialogue in which all parties come to the table under common expectations of being treated as moral equals. Human rights are universal not as a vernacular of cultural prescription but as a language of moral empowerment. Their role is not in defining the content of culture but in trying to enfranchise all agents so that they can freely shape that content.

A case study[20]

Internal and cross-cultural legitimacy for human rights standards needs to be developed. To explain this Ahmed draws support from an example of the right not to be subjected to cruel, inhuman, or degrading treatment or punishment. Insiders may consider certain types of punishment, for example, as dictated or at least sanctioned by norms of a particular cultural tradition as in tandem with law and just behaviour, whereas to outsiders to that culture, the same measures may constitute cruel, inhuman, or degrading treatment. Which position should be taken for setting the standards for such human rights?

All individuals or groups within a society do not hold identical views on the meaning and implications of cultural values and norms, or share the same evaluation of the legitimacy of human rights standards. Dominant groups or classes within the society normally maintain perceptions and interpretations that are supportive of their own interests, proclaiming them to be only a valid view of that culture. Dominated groups or classes may hold different perceptions that are helpful to their struggle to achieve justice for themselves. This is however an *internal struggle* for control over cultural sources and symbols of power within the society. Outsiders, in a bid to help the groups with which they sympathise, claiming to know what valid view of the culture of the society is, would not accomplish the desired effect since it may portray them as agents of an alien culture.

The cultural legitimacy thesis accepts the existing international standards while seeking to enhance their cultural legitimacy within the major traditions of the world through internal dialogue and struggle to establish enlightened perceptions and interpretations of cultural values and norms. Having achieved an adequate level of legitimacy within each tradition, through this internal stage, human rights scholars and advocates should work for cross-cultural legitimacy so that people of diverse cultural traditions can agree on the meaning, scope, and methods of implementing these rights. Instead of being content with the existing least common denominator, it is needed to broaden and deepen universal consensus on the formulation and implementation of human rights through internal reinterpretation of, and cross-cultural dialogue about, the meaning and implications of basic human values and norms.[21]

- *Cultural Relativity and Human Rights*

Culture is defined in a variety of ways in different contexts.[22] For the purpose of this essay, culture is taken in its widest meaning—that of the "totality of values, institutions and forms of behaviour transmitted within society, as well as the material goods produced by man [and woman],this wide concept of culture covers *weltanschauung* [world view], ideologies and cognitive behaviour.[23]

Culture is therefore, the source of the individual and communal world view: it provides both the individual and the community with the values and interests to be pursued in life, as well as the legitimate means for pursuing them. This interpretation can explain peoples' ethnocentricity, the tendency to regard one's own race or social group as the model of human experience or a norm.

A degree of ethnocentricity is unavoidable, indeed indispensable. Even the most radical "dissidents" rely on their culture for survival.[24] Rigid ethnocentricity, however, breeds intolerance and hostility to societies and persons that do not conform to our models and expectations.

The appreciation of our own ethnocentricity should lead us to respect the ethnocentricity of others. Enlightened ethnocentricity would therefore concede the right of others to be "different", whether as members of another society or as individuals within the same society. In sociological terms, this orientation is commonly known as cultural relativism, that is to say, the acknowledgement of equal validity of diverse patterns of life.[25] It stresses "the dignity inherent in every body of custom, and the need for tolerance of conventions though they may differ from one's own.[26]

- *Cultural Universality and Human Rights*

International peace and cooperation are possible and easily achievable if there is a certain minimum cultural consensus on goals and methods. As applied to cooperation in the protection and promotion of human rights, this view means that developing cross-cultural consensus in support of treaties and compacts is desirable. *This consensus can be achieved through internal cultural discourse and cross-cultural dialogue.* This direction may include support for the proponents of enlightened perceptions and interpretations within culture.

One of the apparent paradoxes of culture is the way it combines stability with dynamic continuous change.[27] Change is induced by internal adjustments as well as external influences. Both types of change, however, must be justified through culturally approved mechanisms and adapted to pre-existing norms and institutions. Otherwise, the culture would lose the coherence and stability that are vital for its socialising and other functions.[28]

The object of internal discourse and cross-cultural dialogue is to agree on a body of beliefs to guide action in support of human rights in spite of disagreement on the justification of those beliefs. We should be realistic in our expectations and pursue the maximum possible degree of agreement at whatever level it can be achieved. This approach can be illustrated by the following case study shows that the meaning of the human right is 'not to be subjected to cruel, inhuman or degrading treatment or punishment'.

- *Cruel, Inhuman, or Degrading Treatment or Punishment*

Some international human rights instruments stipulate that "no one shall be subjected to torture or to cruel, inhuman, or degrading treatment or punishment".[29] There is an obvious overlap between the two main parts of this right, i.e., between protection against torture and protection against inhuman or degrading treatment or punishment. For example torture has been defined as constituting "an aggravated and deliberate form of cruel, inhuman or degrading treatment or punishment".[30] But simultaneously, according to the definition of torture adopted in the UN instruments, it "does not include pain or suffering arising only from, inherent in or incidental to lawful sanctions". In other words lawful sanctions can constitute "cruel, inhuman or degrading treatment or punishment".

Here the question dealt with is how to identify the criteria by which lawful sanctions can be held to violate the prohibition of cruel, inhuman or degrading treatment or punishment. The case of the Islamic punishments will be used to illustrate the application of the cross-cultural perspective to this question.

The early history of what now is Article 7 of the Covenant on Civil and Political Rights indicates that drafters and delegates were particularly concerned with preventing the recurrence of atrocities such as those committed in concentration camps during World War II.[31] But at the time of drafting and subsequently no attention was paid to the point that what may be seen as "cruel, inhuman or degrading" in one culture may not be seen in the same light in another culture. Would a cross-cultural approach be helpful in this regard?

Islamic law, commonly known as Shari'a, has never been formally enacted, but the jurists systematised and rationalised what was already accepted as will of God, and developed techniques for interpreting divine sources and for supplementing their provisions where they were silent.[32] Islamic criminal law, as derived from the primary sources because of lack of codification, may be briefly explained as follows.[33] Criminal laws are classified into three main categories; *Hudud, jinayat*and *ta'zir.* The punishments under these heads varied from amputation of limbs for crimes like theft to theory of exact retribution (an eye for an eye) for causing bodily harm. The question being raised here is: Are Muslims likely to accept the repudiation of these punishments *as a matter of Islamic law* on the ground that they are cruel, inhuman, or degrading?

Shari'a criminal law has been displaced by secular criminal law in most Muslim countries. Countries like Saudi Arabia, however, have always maintained Shari'a as their official criminal law. Other countries, such as Iran, Pakistan, and Sudan, have recently reintroduced Shari'a criminal law. There is much controversy over many aspects of the criminal law of Shari'a that raise human rights concerns, including issues of religious discrimination in the application of Shari'a criminal law on non-Muslims,[34] even when Quranic punishments are essentially religious in nature.

From religious point of view, as per the belief held in Islam, human life does not end at death, but extends beyond that to the next life. In the next *eternal* life, every human being will stand judgment and suffer the consequence of his or her actions in this life. A religiously sanctioned punishment, however, will absolve an offender from punishment in the next life because God does not punish twice for the same offence. To people who hold this belief, however severe the Quran punishment may appear to be, it is in fact extremely lenient and merciful in comparison to what the offender will suffer in the next life should the religious punishment not be enforced in this life.[35] Neither internal Islamic reinterpretation nor cross-cultural dialogue is likely to lead to the total abolition of this punishment as a matter of Islamic law. Much can be done, however, to restrict its implementation in practice. For example, there is room for developing stronger general social and economic prerequisites and stricter procedural requirements for the enforcement of the punishment.

Cross-cultural dialogue may also be helpful in this regard. In the Jewish tradition, for instance, jurists have sought to restrict the practical application of equally harsh punishment by stipulating strict procedural and other requirements.[36] This theoretical Jewish jurisprudence may be useful to Muslim jurists and leaders seeking to restrict the practical application of Quranic punishments.

- *Conclusion: Toward a Cross-Cultural Approach*

The question, whether lawful sanctions can be condemned as cruel, inhuman, or degrading punishment or treatment, presents human rights advocates with a serious dilemma. On one hand it is necessary to safeguard the personal integrity and human dignity of the individual against excessive or harsh punishments. On the other hand, it is extremely important to be sensitive to the dangers of cultural imperialism, whether it is a product of colonialism, a tool of international economic exploitation and political subjugation, or simply a product of extreme ethnocentricity. External imposition is not the only option available to human rights advocates. Greater consensus on international standards for protection of individual can be achieved through internal cultural discourse and cross-cultural dialogue.

If one reflects on the interpretation she or he would like to make a norm, it will probably be the one set by the person's culture. Further reflection on how one would feel about the interpretation set by another culture should illustrate the non-tenability of this position. For example, a North American may think that a short term of imprisonment is the appropriate punishment for theft, and wish that to be the universal punishment for this offence. A Muslim, on the other hand, may feel that the amputation of the hand is appropriate under certain conditions and after satisfying strict safeguards. Thinking of making any of these perceptions a universal norm would lead to disagreements from both the sides. Here the point is not to discuss which standard is more correct but to come to an understanding that agreeing on a universal standard may not be as simple as we may think or wish.

In accordance with the proposed approach, the standard itself should be the product of internal discourse and cross-cultural dialogue. Moreover, genuine total agreement requires equal commitment to internal discourse and equally effective participation in cross-cultural dialogue by the adherents or members of different cultural traditions of the world. In view of significant social and political differences and disparities in levels of economic development, some cultures are unlikely to provide equal participation. These processes require certain degree of political liberty, stability, and social maturity, as well as technological capabilities that are lacking in some parts of the world.

Harmonisation

To harmonise the two conflicting theories the concept of acceptance of International instrument with reservation came into practice. For example, Article 16 of Committee on the Elimination of Discrimination against Women talks about compulsory registration of marriage. Government of India expressed reservation on the ground that it is the matter of personal law and government cannot make legislation on the same.

Jack Donnelly supported and actually propounded this theory of harmonising the two extreme viewpoints. He said that *despite striking and profound international differences in ideology, levels and styles of economic development and pattern of political evolution virtually all states today have embraced in speech if not in deed the human rights standards enunciated in Universal Declaration of Human Rights and International Human Rights Covenants*[37].

So, the debate between universalism and relativism is a non-issue. Universal goals and cultural sensitivities can be reconciled in the establishment of realistic strategies to promote human rights. In the words of Jack Donnelly the world should strive to achieve relative universality of Human Rights.

In the process of globalisation there was need for global human rights regime which leads the formation of following international institutions and covenants:

International Bill of Rights:

International Bill of Rights consists of the following three documents, namely—

1. Universal Declaration of Human Rights.
2. International Covenant on Civil and Political Rights.
3. International Covenant on Economic, Social and Cultural Rights.

- *The Universal Declaration of Human Rights, (1948)*

By 1948, the United Nations' new Human Rights Commission had captured the world's attention. Under the dynamic chairmanship of Eleanor Roosevelt—President Franklin Roosevelt's widow, a human rights champion in her own right and the United States delegate to the UN—the Commission set out to draft the document that became the Universal Declaration of Human Rights. Roosevelt, credited with its inspiration, referred to the Declaration as the international Magna Carta for all mankind. It was adopted by the United Nations on December 10, 1948.

This declaration implies the universal recognition of the human rights. This is the milestone in the journey of the development of the human rights. Root (source) of this declaration can be located in the Charter of the United Nations. It is a comprehensive document on the promotion and protection of human rights at global level. The declaration contains thirty articles which deal with various aspects of human rights.

For common understanding of these rights and freedom is of the greatest importance and it can be divided into following parts:[38]

- *Positive rights of human beings*

The articles of the declaration lay down positive rights of individuals. These rights can be divided into four categories:

(a) Those dealing with the personal freedom contained in Articles 1 to 20.

(b) Those dealing with the political rights to form government of their choice contained in Article 21.

(c) Those dealing with the social rights contained in Articles 22 to 28.

(d) The universal declaration also enumerates certain duties as limitation of these rights and freedom in Article 29 provided that: (1) everyone has duties to the community in which alone the free and full development of his personality is possible. (2) In the exercise of his rights and freedoms, everyone shall be subject only to such limitations as are determined by law solely for the purpose of securing due recognition and respect for the rights and freedoms of others and of meeting the just requirements of morality, public order and the general welfare in a democratic society. (3) These rights and freedoms may in no case be exercised contrary to the purposes and principles of the United Nations.

- *International Covenant on Civil and Political Rights, (1966)*

The covenant on civil and political rights, 1966 (ICCPR) has been divided into VI parts containing 53 Articles. In **PART I** only Article 1 has been included. It included the right of people to self-determination. By virtue of that right they can freely determine their political status and freely pursue their economic, social and cultural rights. The government of India acceded to the ICCPR and ICESCR by instrument of Accession signed on 27th march, 1979.[39]

PART II of the covenant contains 4 Articles i.e. Articles 2 to 5. This part enumerates various obligations to ensure that all the citizens are provided as per their rights under the document, by their respective States without discrimination of any kind. According to Robertson, subject to certain exceptions, the covenants "impose on state parties the obligation to maintain a defined standard. They shall take necessary steps, in accordance with its constitutional processes to adopt such legislative or other measures as may be necessary to give effect to rights recognised in the covenant.

PART III of the covenant sets out the various rights from Articles 6 to 27, which are to be protected by law. It provides for all the substantive rights that form the main body of the text. They are the right to life i.e. no one shall be arbitrarily deprived of his life, and that sentence of death may be imposed for most serious crimes. **Article** 7 provides that no one shall be subjected to torture or to cruel, inhuman or degrading treatment or punishment. In particular, no one shall be subjected without his free consent to medical or scientific experimentation. The covenant has further extended protection against retroactive criminal legislation[40] which includes right to recognition as a person before the law,[41] andright against arbitrary or unlawful interference with his privacy.[42]

PART IV of the ICCPR, 1966 (Articles 28 to 45) has a detailed description of the implementation procedure in case of any complaint of violation of the rights mentioned. It provides for establishment of a Human Rights committee as an implementation organ. The commission shall consist of eighteen members.[43] The Committee shall be composed of nationals of the State Parties of high moral character and recognised competence in the field of human rights, consideration being given to the usefulness of the participation of some persons having legal experience.[44] The members of the Committee shall be elected and shall serve in their personal capacity.[45]

PART V of the ICCPR, 1996 contains two article i.e. Articles 46 and 47 and provide for the interpretation of the covenant.

PART VI of the ICCPR, 1996 deals with necessary provision from Article 48 to Article 53 about the signature by the state members of the UN or its specialised agencies, ratification, accession and entering into force, amendment in the covenant to all states by the Secretary-General of the UN.[46]

- *International Covenant on Economic, Social and Cultural Rights (1966)*

The Covenant starts with a Preamble followed by thirty-one articles that are divided into five parts:

Part 1: recognises the right of all people to self-determination as under the covenant on civil and political rights.

Part 2: establishes the principle of progressive realisation. It also requires the rights be recognised without discrimination of any kind.

Part 3: forms the main body of the covenant having the various rights enumerated in the document, such as work, under "just and favourable conditions, right to form and join trade unions, social security, including social insurance, family life, including paid parental leave and the protection of children, etc.

Part 4: provides for the reporting procedure through reporting and monitoring process.

Part 5: governs ratification, entry into force, and amendment of the Covenant.

- *International Convention on the Elimination of All Forms of Racial Discrimination*

It came into force on 4th January, 1969 and by now has been ratified by more than 140 states. It represents the most comprehensive UNITED NATIONS statement regarding discrimination on the grounds of 'race, colour, descent of national or ethnic origin'. State parties to the convention undertake to pursue a policy of elimination of racial discrimination in all its forms and to ensure the protection of special racial groups, guaranteeing their members full and equal enjoyment of human rights and fundamental freedom.

The implementation of the convention is done by a committee on the Elimination of Racial Discrimination **(CERD).** This committee comprising of eighteen independent experts, established under Article 8 of the convention, supervises governmental compliance. The committee has several functions like examination of periodic reports from state parties for implementation of convention.

Some states have made provisions for this convention under their domestic laws and have categorised racial discrimination as a punishable offence, they have even established educational programmers and new agencies to deal with problems of racial discrimination.

Conclusion

The Vienna Declaration (1993) states that:

All human rights are universal, indivisible and interdependent and interrelated. The international community must treat human rights globally in a fair and equal manner, on the same footing, and with the same emphasis. While the significance of national and regional particularities and various historical, cultural and religious backgrounds must be borne in mind, it is the duty of States, regardless of their political, economic and cultural systems, to promote and protect all human rights and fundamental freedoms. (Section 5, Part 1).[47]

This is the latest consensus among States on the issue of universality and culture. It is supposed to embody a compromise on the diverging views of States on the nature of human rights and the cultural peculiarities (among other differences) of societies. It reaffirms the universality of human rights and at the same time takes account of the actual realities existing within each State.

This provision is a clue to where an examination of the present issue must lead. It is a formal basis, at least, of an assumption that States in the Asia-Pacific region are not contesting the premise that human rights are universal which can relate to the specific situations of countries.

There remains an issue on whether such an international statement of agreement is translated into concrete policies, programs and activities in the different countries in the region.

In a regional conference held recently, several Asia-Pacific countries declared support for human rights education that draws "*... on the rich cultural heritage and diversity in the region, including appropriate recognition of family and community values.*" *The same* *declaration states that "... human rights education must affirm not only rights and freedoms but also responsibilities should promote the values and practices of healing, reconciliation and conflict resolution and cultivate participative values of governance, consensus building and accountability".*[48]

Thus, it can be said with a sense of achievement that the idea that Human Rights are indeed the most inalienable rights of every individual is not debatable today. The issue concerning the activists and advocates of Human Rights is agreeing upon the universally acceptable mechanism to find out the standard with which we should consider a moral and cultural sanction for something to be called as Human Right. Though being a herculean task, it has been started with full force and with more and more nations participating it seems to be an achievable task.

References

1. Extract from the Speech by Eleanor Roosevelt on the occasion of adoption of United Nations General Assembly resolution 217 (III) of 10 December 1948. See. Eleanor Roosevelt and the Universal Declaration of Human Rights, *available at:* http://womenshistory. about.com/od/1stladyroosevelte/a/human rights.htm (Visited on November 17, 2013).
2. John O' Manique, "Development, Human Rights and Law", 14(3) *Human Rights Quarterly*, 385 (1992).
3. Hydervali B., "The Jurisprudence of Human Rights" XXX (4) *Indian Bar Review* 25 (2003).
4. *Ibid.*
5. Justice Y.K. Sabharwal, "Human Rights and International Law" available on www.supremecourtof india.nic.in/speeches/speeches_2006/mp.pdf visited on September 2, 2013.
6. Maurice Cranston quoted in. L.J. Macfarlane, *The Theory and Practice of Human Rights* 7 (Temple Smith, London, 1985).
7. Jack Donnelly, "Cultural Relativism and Universal Human Rights" 406 (1984)6 Human Rights Quarterly.
8. Durga Das Basu and Sanwat Raj Bhansali, *Human Rights in Constitutional Law 5 (Lexis NexisButterworths, Wadhwa, Napur, 1994).*
9. Bennet, *International Organisations 258 (Prentice-Hall International, 1991).*
10. Noel A. Kinsella, " Magna Carta for all humanity" 12 *Military Law Journal* 34 (1998).
11. *Ibid.*

12. Fazal M.A., "Drafting a British Bill of Rights" 3 *Journal of Indian Law Institute* 27 (1985).
13. H.O. Agarwal, *International Law and Human Rights* (Central Law Publications, 15th edn., Allahabad, 2008) at 671.
14. Scgwartz Bernard, "American Bill of Rights", 4 *Civil and Military Law Journal* 14 (1978).
15. S.K. Kapoor, *International Law and Human Rights* (Central Law Agency, 14th edn., Allahabad, 2002).
16. H.O. Agarwal, *International Law and Human Rights* (Central Law Publications, 15th edn., Allahabad, 2008).
17. *Id at 749.*
18. Michael Ignatieff, "The Attack on Human Rights", *Foreign Affairs*, Vol. 80, No. 6 (Nov-Dec., 2001), pp. 102-116, (Council on Foreign Relations).
19. *Ibid.*
20. Abdullahi Ahmed An-Na'im, "Toward a Cross-Cultural Approach to Defining Standards of Human Rights—The Meaning of Cruel, Inhuman, or Degrading Treatment or Punishment, *Human Rights in Cross-Cultural Perspectives-A Quest For Consensus*, ed. Abdullahi Ahmed, (University of Pennsylvania Press) 1991.
21. *ibid.*
22. See, for example, T.S.Eliot, *Notes Toward the Definition of Culture(London: Faber and Faber, 1948;* Raymond Williams, *Keywords : A Vocabulary of Culture and Society (*New York: Oxford University Press, 1976), 76-82.
23. Roy Preiswerk, "The of Intercultural Relations in the Study of International Relations," The Year Book of World Affairs 32 (1978): 251
24. Melville Herskovits, *Man and his Works* (New York: Knopf, 1950), 54.
25. See generally, Ruth Benedict, *Patterns of Culture* (Boston: Houghton Mifflin, 1959).
26. Melwille Herskovits, *Man and His Works* (New York: Knopf, 1950), 76.
27. Herskovits, supra note 25, at 4 and 6.
28. See, supra note 21.
29. Article 5 of UDHR of 1966. The latter adds that "In particular, no one shall be subjected without his free consent to medical or scientific experimentation." For the texts of these instruments*see Basic Documents on Human Rights,* ed. Brownlie, 2nd ed. (Oxford; Clarendon Press, 1981), 21 and 128, respectively.
30. Article 1.2 of the Declaration on the Protection of all Persons From Being Subjected to Torture and Other Cruel, Inhuman or Degrading Treatment or Punishment of 1975.
31. M. J. Bossuyt, *Guide to 'Travaux Preparatories' of the International Covenant on Civil and Poilitical Rights* [heienafter cited as Bossuyt, Guide] Dordrecht: Martinus Nijhoff, 1987, 151.

32. On the sources and development of Shari'a *see genarally,* Abdulliah A. An-Na'im, *Toward an Islamic Reformation: Civil Liberties, Human Rights and International Law* (Syracuse: Syracuse University Press, 1990), chap. 2.
33. For fuller explanations see, generally, *ibid*, chap 5; Mohamed S. Elawa, *Punishment in Islamic Law (*Indianapolis: American Trust Publications, 1982); and Safia M. Safwat, "Offences and Penalties in Islamic Law" *Islamic Quarterly, 26 (*1982) :1449.
34. An-Na'im, supra note 43, at 114-18 and 131–33.
35. See, supra note 21.
36. *Encyclopaedia Judaica* (Jerusalem: Keter 1971(), vol 5, 142-47; Vol 6, 991-93.
37. Jack Donnelly, '*Cultural Relativism and Universal Human Rights*', Human Rights Quarterly, Vol. 6, No.4, Nov. 1984.
38. S.R.Bhansali, *Law Relating to Human Rights In International and National Laws and Constitutions, (*Universal Law Publishing Co., New Delhi, 2013).
39. *Ibid.*
40. Article 15
41. Article 16
42. Article 17
43. Article 28(1)
44. Article 28(2)
45. Article 28(3)
46. Supra note 38.
47. JanuszSymonides (ed.), *New Dimensions and challenges for Human Rights* 26 (Ashgate, Dartmouth, 1998).
48. Conference-Workshop on Asia-Pacific Human Rights Education for Development , held in Manila, Philippines in December 1995.

Attachment to Chapter 1: A brief survey of Caste based violence over the decades

This section attempts to highlight the cultural aspect behind caste based violence and tracks the trend of more than sixty years right from the 1950s till 2014. It emerges from the collections of the cases mentioned in this section that not much has changed in the past six and a half decades. This section does not claim to have covered all incidences of caste based violence and even admits to have missed out on certain extremely grave incidences, yet the aim here is not to present a comprehensive history of caste based violence in India, but to:

1. Highlight the cultural roots of such violence and
2. Establish the fact that the nature of such violence has not essentially changed over the past six and a half decades

Notice that the various cases given below, of atrocities against scheduled castes are spread across time and region in the country. Also, notice that the nature of atrocities are also more or less similar and of particular types across region and time. The sociologist N.D. Kamble(1981, pp. 8-46)[1] has given multiple examples of offences against the Scheduled castes, some of them are given below:

June 1951: A village in Himachal Pradesh.

A conference of Scheduled Castes is attacked by Rajput Landlords. The SCs are beaten up with sticks, their leaders tied up with ropes and confined to a cattle pound.

> **June 1952:** A village in the Madurai district of Madras State.
>
> A SC youth asks for tea in a glass at a local shop. Tradition entitles him only to a disposable coconut shell. When he persists, he is kicked and hit on the head by caste Hindus.
>
> **May 1959:** A village in Ahmednagar district of Bombay State.
>
> A Buddhist Marriage party is not allowed to enter the hamlet through the village gates. When they persist, caste Hindus attack them with stones and swords.
>
> **October 1960:** A village in Aurangabad District of Maharashtra.
>
> Caste Hindus enter the Scheduled Caste hamlet and break a statue of Buddha into tiny pieces.

Around 1969-71 Dr Mumtaz Ali Khan studying the nature of cast discriminations in Solur and adjacent areas of Karnataka found that despite being able to afford the luxuries of the newly opened hotels, many a times people belonging to the scheduled castes were not allowed to enter the hotels by the local 'caste Hindus' (Khan, 1971, pp. 153–157). Here too cases of the police officials effecting forced compromise have been noted. Consider for example, a peculiar case quoted by Dr. Khan:

> Until 1969, the Scheduled Castes were not allowed to enter the hotels in Solur. The Scheduled castes were made to stand outside and served... In 1969, the middle aged Scheduled Castes who were aware of the legal rights are reported to have forced their entry in to a hotel run by a Lingayat. The proprietor not only refused to allow them but also mustered a reasonable number of the other Hindus to disperse the Scheduled Caste people. A free-for-all battle began. Heavy damage was caused to the hotel property and the hotel was closed down temporarily.
>
> In the meanwhile the caste Hindus planned to finance a local Muslim to start a tea shop and avenge the humiliation they had experienced earlier. The Scheduled Caste people who had maintained good relations with the Muslims thought they would have no problem. But when they were refused entry into the tea shop, they were surprised. After initial differences, they resorted

to forcible entry. The Muslims who had the support of the caste Hindus are reported to have attacked the Scheduled Caste people. There was a pitched battle between these two groups.

After the fight was over, the Muslims and the caste Hindus presented a joint complaint to the local police for trespass and assault. The Scheduled Caste people also wanted to lodge a counter complaint. But the Sub-Inspector effected a compromise and pacified the Muslims and the Lingayats(p. 157).

An excerpt from Guha's writings throws light upon the symbolic nature of the caste violence (Guha, 2007)[2]:

> **1978 Marathwada.** A group of writers and poets who called themselves 'Dalit Panthers' demanded that the university in Aurangabad – The Marathwada University- be named after their great leader B.R. Ambedkar. On 27 July 1978 the demand was finally acceded to. The renaming was bitterly opposed by the dominant Maratha caste. Students declared a bandh in the region's town...Then they spread into the villages, attacking and sometimes burning Dalit Hamlets. An estimated 5000 people, almost all low caste, were rendered homeless. The order to rename the university was withdrawn (Samiti, 1979).

Another riot took place in Agra in 1978 when a procession was taken out on Dr Ambedkar's birthday with his garlanded photo atop an elephant – traditionally considered as the royal transport for Hindu kings. This "...was too much for the upper castes to abide." (Guha, 2007, pp. 534-36). Two weeks of sporadic fighting between the upper and the scheduled castes followed. Finally, the army was called in to restore order (Lynch, 1981).

Later decades have also been marred by similar incidents of atrocities against the Scheduled castes, some of which have been published by M. Subbiah, and B. Malathi(2013):

- In Bathani Tola, Bhojpur in Bihar on 11 July 1996, 21 Dalits were slaughtered by the Ranvir Sena . Among the dead were 11 women, six children and three infants.

- In Laxmanpur Bathe on 1 December 1997, Ranvir Sena gunned down 58 Dalits.
- In the village of Melavalavu, in Tamil Nadu's Madurai district, following the election of a Dalit to the village council presidency, members of a higher-caste group murdered six Dalits in June 1997, including the elected council president, whom they be headed.
- In January 1999 four members of the village panchayat of Bhungar Khera village in Abohar, Punjab, paraded a handicapped Dalit woman, Ramvatidevi naked through the village. No action was taken by the police.

The study conducted by Indian Social Institute has captured a series of case studies of Dalit repression in the Punjab region during the 1990s upto 2005. In the case study of Talhan Village in Punjab, the incidence of violence against the Ad Dharmis in 2003 is captured (Indian Social Institute, 2005, pp. 83-84). The violence took place because of the reluctance of the upper caste members to have anyone of the Ad Dharmi caste in the management committee of a local village shrine that was collectively owned by the village panchayat. Though the Ad Dharmis formed one of the largest chunk of the village population and had considerable influence in the panchayat elections, they were kept away from certain important activities of the village such as the Gurudwara Committee. "Though it had members from different caste groups, Dalits were never represented in the Commttee". On refusal of the upper caste Jats to include the Ad Dharmis in the committee, the latter approached the local administration and took to the court of law. As a consequence the "non-Ad Dharmi residents of the village were directed not to keep any social or economic relations with the Ad Dharmis. The Jats stopped going to the shops owned by Ad Dharmis in the village and banned them from collecting fodder from their farm" (*ibid.*). (It is to be noticed here that in the concerned region, the Jats are the primary land owners and farmers). "The Ad Dharmis had to either bring fodder from the town or had to collect it from the neighbouring villages. Even the use of village fields for defecating was disallowed." (*ibid.*)

When the Ad Dharmis reached out to Dalit activists in the Jalandhar city and organised protests, violence broke out due to the attempts of the repression of protests by the upper castes. To contain the violence, the police opened fire in which one Dalit was killed. "The tension was so sharp that the local administration had to intervene and had to seal off the village for a couple of days" (*ibid.*).

In the recent past, not much has changed in India as far as caste based discrimination is concerned. Some recent stories still resounds the stories of the past:

> In December 2012 as many as 268 dwellings – huts, tiled-rooves and one or two-room concrete houses of Dalits of the Adi Dravida community near Naikkankottai in Dharmapuri district of western Tamil Nadu were torched by the higher-caste group. The victims alleged this holocaust as 'systematic destruction' of their properties and livelihood resources. (Arivanantham, 2012).
>
> In April 2013, violence broke near Marakkanam (Tamil Nadu) between sections of Dalits and those travelling to Vanniyar gathering at Mamallapuram to attend the annual Chitra Pournami youth congregation at Mamallapuram.. A mob indulged in setting arson to houses and four buses of TNSTC and PRTC. Three people were injured in police firing, one vanniarcader died. Traffic was closed in ECR for a day. (The Hindu, 2013).[3]

Cultural and symbolic issues have been the cause of atrocities and discrimination against scheduled castes in India and is a trend which continues till date. Here is another instance that came to the NCSC from the state of Madhya Pradesh and has also been reported (The Hindu, 2014):

> **June 2014.** A Dalit groom was allegedly forced to get down from the horse he was riding as part of a pre-wedding ritual and beaten up by upper caste men at Sadwa ... Manoj Ahirwar (21) went around the village on horse-back seeking the blessings of village elders, said Chhattarpur's Additional Superintendent of Police (ASP) Neeraj Pandey...As per village "tradition", only upper-caste grooms are "allowed" to ride on a horse, while lower castes have to go on foot to seek the blessings of elders.

> The police said they had arrested seven people identified as Ladle Yadav, KhadiaYadav, AmmuYadav, Mitthu Yadav, JaaharYadav, Ram Singh and Pavrat Pal, while six others, including village headman Khuman Singh, were absconding.
>
> Some persons in the groom's procession also allegedly made some comments leading to the scuffle, with upper caste men objecting to the "violation" of village "tradition".

Similar cases have also occurred in the State of Rajasthan that has been ascribed to the "feudal mentality" by P.L. Mimrothi of the Centre for Dalit Rights (Dhar, The Hindu, 2014):

> **July: 2014.** It was Jaipal's wedding at Gugal Kota in Alwar on June 21. His father, Roshan Lal, made him ride a decorated horse, at the head of the wedding party, to the bride's home. The Rajputs in the village disliked such a celebration by a Dalit family and they would not allow it to go on Mr Jaipal was pulled down from the horse on the road and the guests were attacked. Flying stones hit some of the revellers and some others were beaten up.... Some time back on June 18, another bridegroom, Kamlesh Regar, had been pulled down from his horse at Tarnavonka Kheda in Chittorgarh district. During the wedding season between March and June, nearly a dozen such Ghodi Utaro (pull down from a horse) incidents take place in the State. The upper caste people dislike such celebrations by the Dalits, more so if the bridegroom mounts a horse and goes to the bride's house with band and music."

Other cases of atrocities have been reported, such as the honour killing of a caste Hindu girl marrying a Scheduled Caste man **(The Hindu, June 2014)**; the killing of a man belonging to a scheduled caste for marrying a caste Hindu girl **(The Hindu, May 2014)**; and the raping of a girl belonging to the Scheduled Castes, for his brother's elopement with an upper caste girl and the negligence of the police thereof.

Such cases and many more are relevant not only because they are cases of rape, arson, violence and discrimination but because they have been committed as a result of the cultural antagonisms of certain sections of the society against the Scheduled Castes. Such cases also throw a light on the marked symbolic overtones of the incidents thereby again pointing towards the presence of a strong culture bias against the scheduled castes in India.

Epilogue: Bringing it all together

Post the initial survey of the manuscript, a lot many people have asked me as to how the different chapters of the book are related and despite having slightly touched upon the connectedness of the chapters, I felt that this issue demanded a greater explanation in detail.

To resolve this issue, it would be necessary to understand the reason and the process that went behind the writing of this book. This book came about as a result of long held reflections and conversations that I had with the people of my generation which included people from different backgrounds spread across the country over the course of my work and education in four very distinct states of India – Uttar Pradesh, Rajasthan, Maharashtra and Delhi.

In fact, in order to compile this book, focused group discussions were held at the University of Delhi to understand the various viewpoints of students coming from diverse backgrounds and different places in the nation. An attempt was then made to address the various concerns, questions and perspectives regarding the question of equality in society, thus gathered in these interactions. This book owes much to the perspectives communicated by the student community of the present generation. This was seen as important, as this (the student community) is indeed the section of people who are going to define the future of the country that we live in. They are the ones who are going to impact policies, economic realities and the mind-set of the whole nation in the times to come. They are the people who will define the character of India in the eyes of the world. Hence, it was seen as necessary to understand what the youth of the nation feels about the issues of equality and inter-group conflicts in the country. Therefore, it would not be an exaggeration, if the youth that we interacted with during the course of compilation of the book are indeed regarded as co-authors of this book.

Apart from the youth, learned men and women of the generations above including various academicians, civil servants, professionals and most importantly, social thinkers have been consulted, at times through interactions, and at other times through their writings. Their generations have understood India and shaped its character thus far (and still continue to do so) and these are the people who have thought about, suffered and even at times amended the various social inequalities present across the world.

Coming back to the question of the theme of the book, it is honestly nothing but a confluence of all these diverse viewpoints thus gathered directed towards understanding the following:

- The different types or varieties of inequalities and conflicts that exist in our society (covered in the first three chapters).
- The trends of the past, present and future related to these inequalities and conflicts with reference to the concept of power, which is seen as the fundamental resource in the society. In other words, all inequalities and all conflicts are seen as an inequality of power or as conflicts for power. A trend has been sought to understand how the concentration of power changes over time (in Chapter 4) and how the nature of power changes over time (Chapter 5).
- The role of leadership and individual actions in shaping the course of history – "can an individual positively impact the macro dynamics of the society to end conflict and bring about equality?" "If yes, then how and by adopting which strategies?" (Covered in Chapter 6 of the book).
- Not only in India, but also across the world, what is the role of cross-cultural exposure and dialogue in establishing greater harmony between the various groups of people who inhabit this planet?

Broadly beneath these considerations runs in the under currents, the theme of finding solutions to inequalities and inter-group conflicts.

In fact, this book, as one of the initial readers of the manuscript commented, is a long essay on the theme of understanding a way out of inequalities and inter-group conflicts. Let us now briefly examine each chapter under the light of the above-mentioned theme.

The first chapter titled "Casteism: A problem bygone or a way of life?" begins with the argument that the evil of casteism is one of the long standing artefacts of inequalities and inter-group conflicts in India. The nature of the caste problem is then discussed to understand whether it is a problem of the Hindu Religion? Or is it a rural problem? Or whether it is an economic problem, apolitical problem or a cultural one? Here it is contended that Casteism is essentially a cultural problem with economic roots. However, it is also understood that the economic relevance of the caste system has long outlived its utility (if there was any) and that the culture of caste persists that conversely impacts economic trends. To prove this point, the cases of caste based discriminations in South Asian communities in the United Kingdom have been taken as evidence. These cases point clearly towards the fact that the caste system prevails in Indian, Pakistani, and other South Asian communities even when the members of these communities leave their socio-economic environment and relocate to a foreign land.

The second chapter deals with a second artefact of inequalities and inter-group conflicts in India–Communalism. Different perspectives on the problem of religious conflicts and communalism have been discussed in the second chapter and Dr Bipan Chandra's theory that communalism is above all an ideology that creates a perception of divergence and even opposition of interests between different groups, is elaborated upon.

The third chapter titled "Separatism it is" firstly categorises all the major conflicts in the society as intergroup conflicts and ascribes them to the group forming tendencies and group behaviour of human beings. This chapter argues that human beings can form groups based on any common thread of identity that they share with each other and can thereafter fight with other groups that do not subscribe to their identity. However, the chapter also concludes that the idea that "As long as there will be groups, there shall be conflict" is not necessarily true. Perhaps the most important idea in this chapter is the 3C's model of dealing with or proactively avoiding inter-group conflicts. The 3 C's denote -Contact, Common Goals and Categorisation. According to this model, the 'culture of separatism' or the problem of separatism can only be fought when the 3 Cs are in place—it is only when all the three conditions are fulfilled will conflicting groups become harmonious. The first C stands for contact and it is held that when various groups will be in contact in a neutral environment, they will foster mutual understanding, which will in turn result in greater tolerance towards each other. The second C is Common goals and it is argued that the presence of common goals can bring conflicting groups to come together and do aside with their differences to form a common identity for the sake of survival and/or advancement. Finally, the third C is Categorisation. In simple words, one of the basic prerequisite for harmony to exist is that people define themselves undera superordinate category as "Indians" and not perceive themselves as part of distinct and conflicting identities as"Hindus" or "Muslims". In this manner, this chapter provides a theoretical framework to deal with the problem of inter-group conflicts.

With the fourth chapter, there is a slight turn of emphasis. The fourth and even the fifth chapter are based on the belief that just like all major societal conflicts–whether communal, regional, linguistic, racial or caste based – can be grouped under the umbrella term of 'separatism based inter-group conflicts', similarly, all separatism, inequalities etc. are essentially the result of power dynamics and are in a sense a result of unequal distribution of power. In the fourth chapter it is argued that the concentration of power over the period of history changes in a wave-like form, and that currently we are living in a period wherein more and more people are getting empowered. However, it is also postulated that this may not be a permanent trend and that we have to learn our lessons of distribution of power in the times when the trend is towards greater equality in distribution of power, so as to apply what we have learnt in other times when the situation may not be the same anymore. Essentially this chapter also points towards the fact that while we are moving in a time period where power is getting more and more distributed among groups of people, yet, there are certain groups who have received a disproportionately larger share of power (whether in form of money or political power or knowledge etc.) than the other sections of the society. This has largely been seen as the fundamental cause of intergroup conflicts in the society.

The fifth chapter goes on to argue that apart from the changing trend of concentration of power, there is also a changing trend in the nature of power which has implications for inter-group peace and harmony. According to this chapter, with the phases of history, the meanings of power also change. While in one phase of history, knowledge may be the most important power, in another phase, money or commerce may be the primary source of power. The implication of this chapter is that equality is required not only in terms of providing equal access to money and resources, people need to be brought on a level of parity on the various aspects of power which have been defined as – Knowledge, Coercion (which primarily corresponds to influence in policy formation and legitimacy of rights over the resources of the society), money (or commerce or simply economic resources), and service (or labour or the ability to provide services). Also, this chapter postulates that we are currently in the phase of historical development which lies somewhere between the shift in the primary source of power from commerce to service and a relevant implication of the same is that the ability to provide services or the opportunity to provide services shall be the sphere where most of the inter-group conflicts will take place. When that happens, the same old conflicting groups of caste, religion, region or language will fight among each other in order to be able to vend their services. Hence, policy effort needs to be proactively directed towards creating enough job opportunities or opportunities to allow people to provide their services in the times to come. This along with the application of the 3Cs model could avoid a lot of future inter-group conflicts.

Finally, the sixth chapter titled as "The Role of Leadership: Cases, Stories and Theories" was written to debunk the feeling that may have been aroused in the reader by now that only macro-forces are in control of defining the character of the society and that individuals have no role to play in affecting social outcomes. For this purpose, the role of leaders in resolving social conflicts and reducing social inequalities has been discussed by also taking the leadership of Mahatma Gandhi in bringing together the conflicting sections of the Indian society to win freedom, as a case study. Further, some real life examples borne of the first hand experiences of the writer are discussed to understand exactly what sort of leadership style is most effective in bringing about any change – whether in pursuit of the objective of communal harmony or otherwise. The leadership style pointed out in this regard is strangely no one style at all, but a style based on situational leadership that entails the modification of one's leadership style with respect to situational considerations. Hence, the gist of this chapter is in concluding that macro-forces as well as individual choice and effort, together in interaction, direct the course of history and by implication shall remain important aspects in promoting peace and harmony.

The appendix was added later in the book as some of its initial readers believed that the concerns discussed in this work are not only shared by Indians, but by people around the world. Hence, an additional chapter was added as appendix written with the help of a friend and a post-graduate law student – Upasana Singh. The backbone of this chapter is that cross-cultural understanding, which can be enhanced through dialogues, is most necessary in the formulation of international laws and can positively affect the state of global integration and peace.

Hence, this book is the result of an earnest attempt by the writer to communicate some seemingly complex but inter-related ideas to come up with a holistic sense of the problems that we face as a society and to ponder upon certain solutions regarding the same. Many a times, the reader may still feel that the writer is casually and almost irresponsibly drifting away from the topic, for which the writer only begs solemn apology with the request that such detours of ideas, may be discounted on account of youth or lack of experience, whichever is preferable to the reader. Indeed, this work has been written in an age where ideas are inchoate and before rigidity (and hopefully maturity) sets in with growing age, this opportunity was seized by the writer to pen down his thoughts. Indeed, all that is written in this work may have been and perhaps has been said already by others in their own right, but "since it is written, let it stand" is all that the writer can submit in his defence.

Arpit Chaturvedi

References

1. I have taken the version simplified by Guha, Ramachandra "India After Gandhi: The History of World's Largest Democracy" pp. 380-381.
2. I have simplified and summarised the text.
3. Summarised version of the article (some words have been changed, without changing the essence of the article).

Bibliography

Chapter 1

Joint Stakeholder Report on Caste based Discrimination in India (21st May–`1st June 2012). National Coalition for Strengthening PoA Act Initiation of National Campaign on Dalit Human Rights (NCDHR). 13th Session of the Universal Periodic Review of the UN Human Rights Council.

Ahmad, I. (1978). *Caste and social stratification among Muslims in India.* Manohar.

Amruta, B. (2014, May 1). I had told my son to stay away from Maratha girl, says slain Dalit's mother. *The Hindu.*

Arivanantham, R. (2012, November 8). 3 Dalit colonies face mob fury in Dharmapuri. *The Hindu.*

Deshpande, S., & Bapna, G. (2008). *Dalits in the Muslim and Christian Communities A Status Report on Current Social Scientific Knowledge.* University of Delhi, Department of Sociology. Delhi: National Commission for Minorities.

Dhar, A. (2014, July 14). Dalit wedding fetes face feudal rage in Rajasthan. *The Hindu.*

Gaikwad, R. (2012, December 15). Disabled man falls prey to Muslim caste violence. *The Hindu.*

Gaikwad, R. (2013, August 5). Police turn a blind eye to harassment of minor Dalit girl. *The Hindu.*

Goel, M. L. (2014). *Abbreviated Vita Dr M Lal Goel.* Retrieved December 23, 2014, from University of West California: http://uwf.edu/lgoel.

Guha, R. (2007). *India After Gandhi.* Harper Collins.

Guiso, L., Sapienza, P., & Zingales, L. (2014, December 23). *Does Culture Affect Economic Outcomes?* Retrieved from http://www.kellogg.northwestern.edu/faculty/sapienza/ht

Hoebel, E. (1966). *Anthropology: The study of man* (3d ed.). New York: McGraw-Hill.

Indian Social Institute. (2005). *Social Mobility and Changing Identity – an exploratory study of Dalits in Contemporary Punjab.* Indian Social Institute.

Ingole, K. S. (n.d.). *A Critical Study of Social Exclusion and its Implications.* Retrieved December 23, 2014 from A Dalit Bahujan Media: Dr Babasaheb Ambedkar & his People: http://www.ambedkar.org/research/SOCIAL EXCLUSION and ITS IMPLICATION.pdf

Kamble, N. (1981). *Atrocities on Scheduled Castes in Post-Independent India.* New Delhi: Ashish Publishing House.

Kenneth, K. B. (1996). The Developmental Process. In R. K. Varma, *Sociology of Rural Human Resources* (pp. 1–32). Jaipur, Rajasthan, India: Printwell.

Khan, M. A. (1971). *Scheduled Castes and their Status in India.* University of Michigan: Uppal: 1980.

Lynch, O. M. (1981). Rioting as rational action: An interpretation of the April 1978 riots in Agra. *Economic and political weekly*, 1951-1956.

Mead, G. H. (1934). *Mind, Self and Society.* (C. Morris, Ed.) Chicago: University of Chicago Press.

Metcalf, H., & Rolfe, H. (2010). *Caste Discrimination and harassment in Great Britain.* National Institute of Economic and Social Research. Government of United Kingdom.

National Crime Records Bureau. (2001, 2011, 2013). *Publications: Rate and Percentage Contribution to All India of Crimes Committed Against Scheduled Castes (State, UT-wise & Crime Head-wise – 2001, 2011 & 2013)*. Retrieved November 14, 2014, from National Crime Records Bureau, Ministry of Home Affairs: www.ncrb.gov.in

Office of the Registrar General & Census Commissioner, I. (2001, 2011). *Primary Census Abstract for Total population, Scheduled Castes and Scheduled Tribes.*

Office of the Registrar General & Census Commissioner, India. (2001, 2011). *Primary Census Abstract for Total population, Scheduled Castes and Scheduled Tribes.* Office of the Registrar General & Census Commissioner, India.

Samiti, A. V. (1979). The Marathwada Riots: A Report. *Economic and Political Weekly*, 845–852.

Scuto, G. (2007-08). *Caste Violence in Contemporary India.* Retrieved December 23, 2014 from Dalit Netwerk Nederlan: http://www.dalits.nl/pdf/CasteViolence In ContemporaryIndia.pdf

Sharma, R. S. (2005). The Age of the Rigveda. In *India's Ancient Past* (p. 113). Oxford University Press.

Sharma, S. (2013, December). Hate Crimes in India: An Economic Analysis of Violence and Atrocities Against Scheduled Castes and Scheduled Tribes Delhi, India: Centre for Development Economics, Department of Economics, Delhi School of Economics.

Singh, S. (2009, October 31). Forgotten by all, Belchhi struggles to remember Indira. *The Indian Express*.

Srikrishna, L. (2014, June 26). Woman's marriage with Dalit leads to honour killing. *The Hindu*.

Subbiah, M., & Malathi, B. (2013, June). Caste System and Caste related Violence in Indian Culture. *Indian Journal of Arts, II*(6).

The Hindu. (2013, April 27). Marakkanam violence brings ECR under police surveillance. *The Hindu*.

The Hindu. (2014, June 9). Dalit groom beaten up in M.P. village for riding a horse. *The Hindu.*

Thorat, S., & Sabharwal, N. S. (2010). *Children, Social Exclusion and Development (Working Paper Series, Volume 02, Number 01 – Caste and Social Exclusion: issues related to Concept, Indicators and Measurement.* Retrieved December 23, 2014 from Indian Institute of Dalit Studies: http://www.dalitstudies.org.in/images/stories/Unicef_IIDS_Working_Paper_Volume_2_No1.pdf

Waughray, A. (2009, March). Caste Discrimination: A Twenty-First Century Challenge for UK Discrimination Law? *The Modern Law Review, 72*(2), 182 – 219.

Chapter 2 & Attachment

Anwar, F. (2001). *Nobility Under the Mughals, 1628–1658.* Manohar Publishers & Distributors.

Azad, M. A. (1988). *India Wins Freedom.* Orient Black Swan.

Chandra, B. (1989). The Rise and Growth of Communalism. In B. Chandra, M. Mukherjee, A. Mukherjee, S. Mahajan, & K. N. Panikkar, *India's Struggle for Independence.* Penguin India.

Chandra, B. (2008). *Communalism in Modern India.* Har Anand Publications.

Chandra, S. (2003). *Essays on Medieval Indian History.* Oxford University Press.

Chattopadhyaya, B. (1994). *The Making of Early Medieval India.* Oxford University Press.

De Felice, R. (1977). *Interpretations of Fascism.*Harvard University Press.

Desai, A. R. (2005). *Social Background to Indian Nationalism* (6th ed.). Popular Prakashan.

Dutt, R. P. (n.d.). *India To-Day.* Read Books.

Faruki, Z. (1977). *Aurangzeb and his times.* Al-Biruni.

Felice, R. D. (1995). *The Interpretations of Fascism (Le interpretazioni del fascismo).* Laterza.

Gandhi, M. K. (1926, April 2–July 26). *Collected Works of Gandhi.* Retrieved November 26, 2014 from http://www.gandhiserve.org/cwmg/VOL035.PDF

Gandhi, M. K. (1936, August 15). *A Vindication of Caste by Mahatma Gandhi.* (Columbia University) Retrieved November 26, 2014 from http://ccnmtl.columbia.edu/projects/mmt/ambedkar/web/appendix_1.html

Habib, I. (2013). Questioning's within the Religious Thought: The Experience of Islam. *The K.M. Ashraf Memorial Lecture* (p. 42). Delhi: The History Society, Kirori Mal College, University of Delhi.

Hunter, W. W. (1872). *The Indian Musalmans.* Trübner.

Jones, J. (2008). *Blood That Cries Out From the Earth : The Psychology of Religious Terrorism.* Oxford University Press.

Krishna, K. B. (1939). *The Problem of Minorities, or Communal Representation in India.* London: George Allen And Unwin Ltd.

Nehru, J. (1946). *The Discovery of India.* Oxford University Press.

Pandey, G. (2012). *The Construction of Communalism in Colonial North India.* New Delhi: Oxford University Press.

Prasad, B. (1946). *India's Hindu-Muslim Questions.* London: George Allen and Unwin.

Savarkar, V. D. (n.d.). *Hindutva: Who is a Hindu?* Hindi Sahitya Sadan.

Smith, W. C. (2006). *Modern Islam In India.* Hesperides Press.

Thapar, R. (1996, September-October). Tyranny of Labels. *Social Scientist, 24*(9/10).

Chapter 3

Akerlof, G. A. (2010). *Identity Economics: How Our Identities Shape Our Work, Wages, and Well-Being.* Princeton University Press.

Akerlof, G. A., & Kranton, R. E. (2000, August). Economics and identity. *The Quarterly Journal of Economics*, 715–753.

Akerlof, G. A., & Kranton, R. E. (2005). Identity and the economics of organisations. *Journal of Economic Perspectives*, 9–32.

Allport, G. (1954). Retrieved November 26, 2014, from University of Washington Faculty Web Server: http://faculty.washington.edu/caporaso/courses/203/readings/allport_Nature_of_prejudice.pdf

Ambedkar, B. R. (1936). *The Annihilation of Caste*. Retrieved November 26, 2014 from http://ccnmtl.columbia.edu/projects/mmt/ambedkar/web/index.html

Ball, S., Eckel, C., Grossman, P. J., & Zame, W. (2001, February). Status in markets. *The Quarterly Journal of Economics*, 161–188.

Chandra, B. (1989). The Rise and Growth of Communalism. In B. Chandra, M. Mukherjee, A. Mukherjee, S. Mahajan, & K. N. Panikkar, *India's Struggle for Independence*. Penguin India.

Chen, Y., & Li, S. X. (2009). Group identity and social preferences. *American Economic Review*, 431–57.

Cook, S. W. (1985). Experimenting on social issues: The case of school desegration. *American Psychologist*, 452-460.

Gaertner, S. L., Dovidio, J. F., Anastasio, P. A., Bachman, B. A., & Rust, M. C. (1993). The common ingroup identity model: Recategorisation and the reduction of intergroup bias. *European Review of Social Psychology, 4*(1), 1-26.Gandhi, M. K. (1926, April 2-July 26). *Collected Works of Gandhi*. Retrieved November 26, 2014 from http://www.gandhiserve.org/cwmg/VOL035.PDF

Gandhi, M. K. (1936, August 15). *A Vindication of Caste by Mahatma Gandhi*. (Columbia University) Retrieved November 26, 2014 from http://ccnmtl.columbia.edu/projects/mmt/ambedkar/web/appendix_1.html

Rigveda Samhita, with the commentary of Sayana. (1933-5). (R. T. Gifith, Trans.) Pune: Vaidik Samshodhan Mandal.

Guha, R. (2007). *India After Gandhi.* Harper Collins.

Habib, I. (2013). Questioning's within the Religious Thought: The Experience of Islam. *The K.M. Ashraf Memorial Lecture* (p. 42).

Delhi: The History Society, Kirori Mal College, University of Delhi.

Hilton, D. J., & Liu, J. H. (2008). Culture and inter-group relations: The role of social representations of history. In R. Sorrentino, & S. Yamaguchi (Eds.), *The Handbook of motivation and cognition: The cultural context* (pp. 343–368). New York: Guilford.

Hoff, K., & Pandey, P. (2006, May). Discrimination, social identity, and durable inequalities. *American Economic Review*, 206–211.

Leslie, J. (2003). *Authority and Meaning in Indian Religions: Hinduism and the Case of Vâlmîki.* Ashgate Publishing Ltd.

Lindley, M. (n.d.). *Changes in Mahatma Gandhi's Views on Caste and Intermarriage*. Retrieved November 26, 2014 from Academia.edu: http://www.academia.edu/326347/Changes_in_Mahatma_Gandhi_s_views_on_ caste_and_intermarriage.

Liu, J. H. (2012). *A Cultural Perspective on Intergroup Relations and Social Identity: Online Readings in Psychology and Culture*. Retrieved November 26, 2014, from Scholar Works, Grand Valley State University: http://dx.doi.org/10.9707/2307-0919.1119.

Liu, J. H., & Hilton, D. J. (2005). How the past weighs on the present: Social representations of history and their role in identity politics. *British Journal of Social Psychology* (44), 537–556.

Sharma, R. S. (2005). The Age of the Rigveda. In *India's Ancient Past* (p. 113). Oxford University Press.

Sharma, S. (2013, December). Hate Crimes in India: An Economic Analysis of Violence and Atrocities Against Scheduled Castes and Scheduled Tribes. Delhi, India: Centre for Development Economics, Department of Economics, Delhi School of Economics.

Sherif, M., Harvey, O. J., White, B. J., Hood, W. R., & Sherif, C. W. (1954/1961). *Intergroup Conflict and Cooperation: The Robbers Cave Experiment*. Retrieved November 10, 2014 from Classics in the History of Psychology: http://psychclassics.yorku.ca/Sherif/chap1.htm

Tajfel, H. M. (1971). Social categorisation and intergroup behaviour. *European Journal of Social Psychology*, 149–178.

Thapar, R. (2003). *The Penguin History of Early India: From the Origins to AD 1300.* Penguin.

Turner, M. E., & Pratkanis, A. R. (1998, January 1). Twenty-five years of groupthink theory and research: lessons from the evaluation of a theory. *Organisational Behavior and Human Decision Processes, 73*(23), 105–115.

Varshney, A. (2001). Ethnic Conflict and Civil Society India and Beyond. *World Politics, 53*(3), 362–398.

Chapter 4

Akerlof, G. A. (2010). *Identity Economics: How Our Identities Shape Our Work, Wages and Well-Being.* Princeton University Press.

Akerlof, G. A., & Kranton, R. E. (2000, August). Economics and identity. *The Quarterly Journal of Economics*, 715–753.

Akerlof, G. A., & Kranton, R. E. (2005). Identity and the economics of organisations. *Journal of Economic Perspectives*, 9–32.

Albernethy, G. L. (1959). *The Idea of Equality.* Richmond: John Knox.

Ali, M. A. (2001). *The Mughal nobility under Aurangzeb.* Oxford University Press.

Anwar, F. (2001). *Nobility Under the Mughals (1628–1658) (South Asian studies/South Asia Institute, New Delhi Branch, Heidelberg University).* Delhi: Manohar Publishers and Distributors.

Arneson, R. (1989). Equality and Equal Opportunity for Welfare. *Philosophical Studies*(56), 77–93.

Ball, S., Eckel, C., Grossman, P. J., & Zame, W. (2001, February). Status in markets. *The Quarterly Journal of Economics*, 161–188.

Barnett, V. (1998). *Kondratiev and the Dynamics of Economic Development: Long Cycles and Industrial Growth in Historical Context.* London: Macmillan.

Bedau, H. A. (1967). Egalitarianism and the Idea of Equality. In J. R. Pennock, & J. C. (eds.), *Equality* (pp. 3–27). New York: Atherton.

Benn, S. I. (1959). *Social Principles and the Democratic State.* London: Allen & Unwin.

Borland, E. (2008). Class consciousness. In V. N. Parrillo, *Encyclopaedia of social problems* (Vol. I, p. 134). SAGE.

Brighouse, H., & Swift, A. (2009). Legitimate Parental Partiality. *Philosophy and Public Affairs*(37), 43–80.

Brown, H. P. (1988). *Egalitarianism and the Generation of Inequality.* Oxford: Clarendon.

Callinicos, A. (2000). *Equality.* Oxford: Polity Press.

Chen, Y., & Li, S. X. (2009). Group identity and social preferences. *American Economic Review*, 431–57.

Chernyshevsky, N. (1989). *What is to be Done?* (1 ed.). (W. G. Wagner, Ed., & M. B. Katz, Trans.) Cornell University Press.

Cruz, J. (2006). *Patterns of Middle Class Conduct in Nineteenth-Century Spain and Latin America: The Role of Emulation.* Retrieved December 6, 2014 from University of Delaware: http://www.iga.ucdavis.edu/Research/All-UC/conferences/2006-fall/Cruz.pdf.

Farooqui, A. (2001). *Early Social Formations.* Delhi: Manak Publications Pvt Ltd.

Fishkin, J. (1983). *Justice, Equal Opportunity, and the Family.* New Haven: Yale University Press.

Habib, I. (1972). The System of Bills of Exchange (*Hundis*) in the Mughal Empire. *Indian History Congress*, (pp. 290–303). Muzaffarpur.

Haider, N. (2002). The Monetary Basis. In A. K. Bagchi, *Money and Credit in Indian History, From Early Medieval Times* (pp. 58–83). Delhi.

Hajdin, M. (2001). *The Notion of Equality.* Aldershot: Ashgate.

Hay Group. (2005). *Hay Job Evaluation: Foundations and Applications*. Retrieved December 6, 2014 from Hay Group Web Site: http://www.haygroup.com/downloads/ww/wp-Job_Evaluation.pdf

Heller, H. (2006). *The Bourgeois Revolution in France, 1789–1815.* Berghahn Books.

Hoff, K., & Pandey, P. (2006, May). Discrimination, social identity, and durable inequalities. *American Economic Review*, 206–211.

Hofstede, G. (2001). *Culture's Consequences: comparing values, behaviours, institutions, and organisations across nations* (2nd ed.). SAGE Publications.

Khan, I. A. (1968, April). The Nobility under Akbar and the Development of his Religious Policy, 1560-80. *The Journal of the Royal Asiatic Society of Great Britain and Ireland*, 29–36.

Lenin, V. I. (1987). *Essential Works of Lenin: "What is to be Done?" and Other Writings.* Dover Publications.

Locke, J. (1690). *Second Treatise of Government* (1980 edition ed.). (C. B. MacPherson, Ed.) Indianapolis: Hackett.

Machiavelli, N. (1532). *The Prince.* Penguin UK (30 June 2011).

Mandelbrot, B., & Hudson, R. L. (2004). *The (mis)behaviour of markets : a fractal view of risk, ruin, and reward.* New York: Basic Books.

Marx, K. (n.d.). *Essential Writings of Karl Marx: Economic and Philosophic Manuscripts, Communist Manifesto, Wage Labor and Capital, Critique of the Gotha Program* [1st (March 31, 2010) ed.]. Red and Black Publishers.

Mas-Colell, A., Whinston, M. D., & Green, J. R. (1995). *Microeconomic Theory.* New York and Oxford: Oxford University Press.

McPhee, P. (2002). *The French Revolution, 1789–1799* (First Paperback Edition ed.). Oxford University Press.

Milkovich, G. T., & Newman, J. M.-W. (2005). Job Analysis; Evaluating Work: Job Evaluation. In *Compensation* (8th ed., pp. 85–146). McGraw Hill Higher Education.

Mosca, G. (n.d.). *The Ruling Class.* Nabu Press.

Nove, A. (1990). *An Economic History of the USSR.* Penguin Book.

Pareto, V. (n.d.). *The Transformation of Democracy (Social Science Classics Series).* (C. Powers, Ed.) Transaction Publishers.

Parkinson, C. (1841). On the present condition of the labouring poor in Manchester. In *Documents of the Industrial Revolution 1750-1850: Select Economic and Social Documents for Sixth forms (Economic History)* [Reprint (2006) ed., p. 160]. Routledge.

Pipes, R. (2001). *Communism: A History* [Reprint edition (5 August 2003) ed.]. Modern Library.

Prakash, O. (1987). Foreign Merchants and Indian Mints in the Seventeenth and Early Eighteenth Century. In J. F. Richards, *The Imperial Monttary System of Mughal India* (pp. 171–192). Delhi.

Roemer, J. E. (1998). *Equality of Opportunity.* Cambridge: Harvard University Press.

Sinha, A. (2010). *Europe in Transition: From Feudalism to Industrialisation.* New Delhi: Manohar Publications.

Skinner, Q. (2013, February 12). How Machiavellian was Machiavelli? England: Youtube.

Steiner, H. (1994). *An Essay on Rights.* Wiley.

Tajfel, H. M. (1971). Social categorisation and intergroup behaviour. *European Journal of Social Psychology*, 149–178.

Thomson, D. (1949). *Equality.* Cambridge: Cambridge University Press.

Chapter 5

Anderson, P. (2013). *Passages From Antiquity to Feudalism.* Verso Books.

Batra, R. (1978). *The Downfall of Capitalism and Communism: a New Study of History.* New York: Macmillan Publishers.

Cruz, J. (2006). *Patterns of Middle Class Conduct in Nineteenth-Century Spain and Latin America: The Role of Emulation.* Retrieved December 6, 2014 from University of Delaware: http://www.iga.ucdavis.edu/Research/All-UC/conferences/2006-fall/Cruz.pdf

Farooqui, A. (2001). *Early Social Formations.* New Delhi: Vijay Chowk Laxmi Nagar.

Galansky, A. (2008, July 5). How power shapes executive choice. (A. Henretty, Interviewer)

Habib, I. (1972). The System of Bills of Exchange (*Hundis*) in the Mughal Empire. *Indian History Congress*, (pp. 290–303). Muzaffarpur.

Haider, N. (2002). The Monetary Basis. In A. K. Bagchi, *Money and Credit in Indian History, From Early Medieval Times* (pp. 58–83). Delhi.

Heller, H. (2006). *The Bourgeois Revolution in France, 1789–1815.* Berghahn Books.

Kahneman, D. (2011). *Thinking, Fast and Slow.* Farrar, Straus and Giroux.

Latané, B., & Darley, J. M. (1970). *The Unresponsive Bystander: Why Doesn't He Help?* Appleton-Century Crofts.

McClelland, D. C. (1987). *Human Motivation.* CUP Archive.

McPhee, P. (2002). *The French Revolution, 1789–1799* (First Paperback Edition ed.). Oxford University Press.

Prakash, O. (1987). Foreign Merchants and Indian Mints in the Seventeenth and Early Eighteenth Century. In J. F. Richards, *The Imperial Monttary System of Mughal India* (pp. 171–192). Delhi.

Sinha, A. (2010). *Europe in Transition: From Feudalism to Industrialisation.* New Delhi: Manohar Publications.

Chapter 6

Basham, A. (2004). The Wonder That Was India.Picador.

Bass, B. M., & Avolio, B. J. (1994). Improving Organisational Effectiveness Through Transformational Leadership. Sage Publications.

Bass, B. M. (1985). Leadership and performance beyond expectations. New York, NY: Free Press.

Bass, B. M. (1990). Bass & Stogdill's handbook of leadership: Theory, research, and managerial applications (3rd ed.). New York, NY, US: Free Press.

Bass, B. M. & Bass, R. (2008). The Bass handbook of leadership: Theory, research, and managerial applications (4th ed.). New York: Free Press.

Blake, R.; Mouton, J. (1964). The Managerial Grid: The Key to Leadership Excellence. Houston: Gulf Publishing Co.

Blyn, G. (1966). Agricultural Trends in India, 1891–1947: Output, Availability, and Productivity.University of Pennsylvania Press.

Brown, J. M. (1974). Gandhi's Rise to Power: Indian Politics 1915–1922 (Cambridge South Asian Studies Volume 11). Cambridge University Press.

Chandra, B. (1989). The Rise and Growth of Communalism. In B. Chandra, M. Mukherjee, A. Mukherjee, S. Mahajan, & K. N. Panikkar, India's Struggle for Independence. Penguin India.

Chandra, B. (2008). Communalism in Modern India. HarAnand Publications.

Chatterjee, P. (1986). Nationalist Thought and the Colonial World: A Derivative Discourse. Zed Books.

Dutt, R. P. (n.d.). India To-Day. Read Books.

F. E. Fiedler, A Theory of Leadership Effectiveness (New York: McGraw-Hill, 1967)

Guha, R. (2007). India After Gandhi. Harper Collins.

Hardiman, D. (1982). Peasant Nationalists of Gujarat: Kheda District, 1917–34. Oxford University Press.

Henningham, S. (1982). Peasant movements in colonial India: North Bihar, 1917–1942. Issue 9 of Australian National University monographs on South Asia.

Hoffman, B. J., Woehr, D. J., Maldagen-Youngjohn, R., & Lyons, B. D. (2011). Great man or greatvmyth? A quantitative review of the relationship between individual differences and leader effectiveness. Journal of Occupational and Organisational Psychology, 84 (2), 347-381.

Judge, T. A., Bono, J. E., Ilies, R., & Gerhardt, M. W. (2002). Personality and leadership: A qualitative and quantitative review. Journal of Applied Psychology, 87(4), 765-780.

Judge, T. A., Colbert, A. E., & Ilies, R. (2004). Intelligence and Leadership: A Quantitative Review and Test of Theoretical Propositions. Journal of Applied Psychology, 89(3), 542-552.

Judge, T. A., Piccolo, R. F., & Kosalka, T. (2009). The bright and dark sides of leader traits, A review and theoretical extension of the leader trait paradigm. The Leadership Quarterly, 20(6), 855–875.

Judge, T. A., Woolf, E. F., Hurst, C., & Livingston, B. (2006). Charismatic and Transformational Leadership, A Review and an Agenda for Future Research. Zeitschriftfür Arbeits-und Organisations psychologie, 50(4), 203-214.

Kumar, R. (1971). Essays on Gandhian politics: the Rowlatt Satyagraha of 1919. Clarendon Press.

McClelland, D. C., & Boyatzis, R. E. (1982). Leadership motive pattern and long-term success in management. Journal of Applied Psychology, 67(6), 737–743.

Parekh, B. C. (2010). Gandhi. Sterling Publishing Company, Inc., 2010.

Parel, A. (2006). Gandhi's Philosophy and the Quest for Harmory. Cambridge University Press.

Sarkar, S. (2001). Modern India: 1885–1947 (Reprint ed.). Macmillan.

Sarkar, S. (n.d.). Towards Freedom: Documents on the Movement for Independence in India.

Yukl G. (2006). Leadership in organisations. Upper Saddle River, NJ: Prentice-Hall.

Yukl, G., & Van Fleet, D. D. (1992).Theory and research on leadership in organisations. Handbook of industrial and organisational psychology, Vol. 3 (2nd ed.). (pp. 147–197). Palo Alto, CA, US: Consulting Psychologists Press.

Zaccaro, S. J. (2001). The nature of executive leadership: A conceptual and empirical analysis of success. Washington, DC, US: American Psychological Association.

Zaccaro, S. J. (2007). Trait-based perspectives of leadership. American Psychologist, 62(1),

Zaccaro, S. J., Kemp, C., & Bader, P. (2004).Leader traits and attributes. The nature of leadership. (pp. 101–124). Thousand Oaks, CA, US: Sage Publications, Inc.

Appendix

Books

1. Maurice Cranston quoted in. L.J. Macfarlane, *The Theory and Practice of Human Rights* 7 (Temple Smith, London, 1985).
2. Jack Donnelly ,*"Cultural Relativism and Universal Human Rights"* 406 (1984)6 Human Rights Quarterly.
3. Durga Das Basu and Sanwat Raj Bhansali, *Human Rights in Constitutional Law* 5 (Lexis Nexis Butter worths, Wadhwa, Napur, 1994).
4. Bennet, *International Organisations* (Prentice-Hall International, 1991).
5. H. O. Agarwal, *International Law and Human Rights* (Central Law Publications, 15th edn., Allahabad, 2008).
6. S.K. Kapoor, *International Law and Human Rights* (Central Law Agency, 14th edn., Allahabad, 2002).
7. H. O. Agarwal, *International Law and Human Rights* (Central Law Publications, 15th edn., Allahabad, 2008).
8. Abdullahi Ahmed An-Na'im, "*Toward a Cross-Cultural Approach to Defining Standards of Human Rights*". The Meaning of Cruel, Inhuman, or Degrading Treatment or Punishment, *Human Rights in Cross-Cultural Perspectives-A Quest For Consensus,* ed. Abdullahi Ahmed, (University of Pennsylvania Press) 1991.

9. T.S.Eliot, *Notes Toward the Definition of Culture (London: Faber and Faber, 1948;* Raymond Williams, *Keywords : A Vocabullary of Culture and Society (*New York: Oxford University Press, 1976).

10. Melville Herskovits, *Man and his Works* (New York: Knopf, 1950).

11. Ruth Benedict, *Patterns of Culture* (Boston: Houghton Mifflin, 1959).

12. M. J. Bossuyt, *Guide to 'TravauxPreparatories' of the International Covenant on Civil and Poilitical Rights.*

13. Abdulliah A. An-Na'im, *Toward an Islamic Reformation: Civil Liberties, Human Rights and International Law* (Syracuse: Syracuse University Press, 1990).

14. S.R.Bhansali, *Law Relating to Human Rights In International and National Laws and Constitutions, (*Universal Law Publishing Co., New Delhi, 2013).

Journals, Articles, and Reviews

1. Justice Y.K. Sabharwal, "*Human Rights and International Law*".

2. John O' Manique, "*Development, Human Rights and Law*", 14(3) Human Rights Quarterly, (1992).

3. Hydervali B., "*The Jurisprudence of Human Rights*" XXX (4) Indian Bar Review 25 (2003).

4. Noel A. Kinsella, " *Magna Carta for all humanity*" 12 Military Law Journal 34 (1998).

5. Fazal M.A., "*Drafting a British Bill of Rights*" 3 Journal of Indian Law Institute 27 (1985).

6. Scgwartz Bernard, "*American Bill of Rights*", 4 Civil and Military Law Journal 14 (1978).

7. Michael Ignatieff, "*The Attack on Human Rights*", Foreign Affairs, Vol. 80, No. 6 (Nov-Dec., 2001) (Council on Foreign Relations).

8. Roy Preiswerk, "The of Intercultural Relations in the Study of International Relations". The Year Book of World Affairs 32 (1978).

9. JanuszSymonides (ed.), *New Dimensions and challenges for Human Rights* 26 (Ashgate, Dartmouth, 1998).

Websites

1. http://womenshistory.about.com/od/1stladyroosevelte/a/human_rights.htm.
2. www.supremecourtof india.nic.in/speeches/speeches_2006/mp.pdf.

Index